JOHN WITHERSPOON

AN AMERICAN LEADER

BY MATTHEW F. ROSE

CONTENTS

CREDITS

EDITOR Alan R. Crippen II
EDITORIAL ASSISTANCE Gina Dalfonzo, Robert Patterson and Lacey Bloom
ART DIRECTOR Amy Fox
DESIGN AND PRODUCTION Amy Fox and Ashleigh Ruther
HISTORICAL AND VISUAL RESEARCH Brian Bunnell, Karen Krugh and
Ashleigh Ruther

INTRODUCTION

In America's federal city, there are hundreds of statues of our nation's heroes. Commissioned as icons of American beliefs, ideals and values, such statues represent the best aspirations of what it means to be an American. Throughout the District of Columbia, various citizens are commemorated with bronze likenesses for their patriotism, valor and fidelity to the universal God-given endowment of the inalienable rights to life, liberty and the pursuit of happiness, expressed in the Declaration of Independence.

At the intersection of Connecticut Avenue, 18th and N Streets in the Northwest section of Washington stands one such statue. Occupying a small grassy island in the middle of three currents of macadam thoroughfares, an impressive bronze monument projects skyward to an approximate height of fifteen feet. Yet as prominent a landmark as the figure is, it is virtually indistinguishable from the scores of other statues throughout the city. Passersby are generally oblivious to its existence. Even were you to ask an area merchant or resident, it is unlikely that they would know the statue's identity. The figure is that of Rev. John Witherspoon (1723-1794), a signer of the Declaration of Independence for the State of New Jersey and a very significant, though largely

John Witherspoon

forgotten, founder of the American republic.

Witherspoon immigrated to America from Scotland in 1768 and became one of the foremost figures in American public life during the Revolutionary period. A Presbyterian minister and president of the College of New Jersey (later Princeton University), Witherspoon epitomizes the confluence of faith and reason, Holy Scripture and natural law, and the evangelically awakened and intellectually enlightened dimensions of the American political order.

Not only did Witherspoon sign the Declaration of Independence (the only practicing clergyman to do so), but he also continued to serve as a member of Congress for six years. During that time he signed the Articles of Confederation, served on 126 committees including the Board of War and Committee on Foreign Affairs, and personally drafted three religious proclamations on behalf of Congress.

These career highlights alone should be enough to secure Witherspoon's place among the epoch-making American founders. His most lasting and significant contribution to the young republic, however, was the moral and intellectual formation of his students at Princeton. Contemporary historian Garry Wills has described Witherspoon as "probably the most influential teacher in

Library of Congress (LC-USZ62-87607)

Unveiled on May 20, 1908, this bronze statue of John Witherspoon stands at a busy Washington intersection as a testament to "the man who shaped the men who shaped America."

the history of American education."[1] From among the 478 students who matriculated at Princeton during his tenure emerged a U.S. president (James Madison), vice president (Aaron Burr), seventy-seven members of Congress and three Supreme Court justices. In addition, 114 graduates became ministers of the Gospel, and nineteen of this number became presidents of leading institutions of higher education in the new American republic.

In the biographical essay that follows, Matthew F. Rose tells Witherspoon's story in a way that is not only informative and inspirational but also provocative, especially for today's religious conservatives. The life of John Witherspoon testifies to the historical reality that the Christian faith was highly influential in shaping early American culture and its political institutions. Mixing religion and politics is a tradition as old as (in fact, older than) the republic itself. For people who are deeply motivated and animated by a Christian vision of and for human life, including political life, the life and thought of John Witherspoon will effect encouragement and confidence. Arguably, Witherspoon was the most evangelical of the founders. Upon reading Mr. Rose's essay, Christians will find comfort in a "communion of the saints" – a shared pilgrimage with Witherspoon of struggling to apply their faith to every walk of life, even political life. Having trod this soil before us, Witherspoon is one of that "great cloud of witnesses."

Specifically, his arguments for "the public interest of religion" are very appropriate for our current circumstances, when the presidency, Congress and the Courts have seemingly lost transcendent moral bearings. In this secularized age, Witherspoon's *Lectures on Moral Philosophy* and his sermons may seem anachronistic. Many people today may be as deaf to his message as they are blind to his statue. But for those of us who believe that constitutional republican democracy is predicated upon the existence of transcendent truth and a permanent moral order, Witherspoon's teaching is as timeless as it was for James Madison and the founding generation under his tutelage. The challenge remains for us to relearn and re-articulate these ideas to a society that has largely forgotten its past and redefined its organizing principles.

The Witherspoon Fellowship at Family Research Council has commissioned this essay to commemorate the life of a great American spiritual,

---

[1] Garry Wills, *Explaining America: The Federalist* (Garden City, N.Y.: Doubleday & Co., 1981), p. 18.

John Witherspoon

intellectual and political leader. Our hope is that this essay will help to spark a renewed scholarly interest in Witherspoon and in the philosophical and theological ideas that informed his life, thought and contribution to the American political order.

Alan R. Crippen II
The Witherspoon Fellowship
Washington, D.C.

JOHN WITHERSPOON

AN AMERICAN LEADER

I t is a daunting task to capture adequately a man who seems to defy classification. So it is with the Reverend John Witherspoon, a man who by force of intellectual acumen and sturdy character both lit and fueled the fire of the American Revolution. With the effortless grace of men of his distinction, Witherspoon wore the hats of parson, pedagogue and patriot. He was the epitome of the well-rounded Scottish Enlightenment man. Congressional records speak of "an able scholar, forceful preacher, a man of public affairs, as well as a fisherman, a golfer and an excellent horseman."[2] In fact, any one of Witherspoon's primary careers would have been enough to preserve his claim to America's roots. But in his mind, the duty of any thoughtful Christian would require as much. The burning zeal for the moral and social well-being of Americans that was his constant, would inspire him to be one of the most eminent men in American history. And it remains for modern Christians – who face many of the same issues Witherspoon himself did – to rekindle his spirit of piety and courage and to dwell upon the whole ministry of his life in the hope of living as Christ would have us live.

---

[2] Dr. Edward L. R. Elson, "A Protestant Reformer and the American Revolution – An Appreciation of John Witherspoon," a sermon delivered at the National Presbyterian Church on October 28, 1962, and entered into the *Congressional Record*, Vol. 122, Part 4 (Book #1348), 94th Congress, 2nd Session, February 19 through March 2, 1976, on p. 3733, by Mr. Henry M. Jackson as supporting documentation for Bill S. 2996.

BEGINNINGS ON THE BONNIE
BANKS OF SCOTLAND

John Witherspoon's roots can be traced back to the rolling hills of Scotland, where in February of 1723 he was born. At the time of John's birth, his father, James (1691-1759), was the minister of Yester and one of King George II's chaplains for Scotland.[3] The Presbyterian parish of Yester had long been fertile ground for the heritage of ministry for which James and the Witherspoon name were renowned. James is invariably portrayed as a man of sundry talents, but one who possessed a combative and tenacious disposition. Immensely erudite, James drew upon his command of French, German and Latin texts to delight his congregations. He was widely lauded for his notable piety and piercing acumen from the pulpit. Indeed, he was said to have been "a man of five talents constitutionally akin to the man of one."[4] Fortunately for posterity, his son John was denied his father's distemper but endowed with his gifts and tastes.[5] Anne Walker, John's mother, also came from a ministerial lineage – the daughter of the minister of Temple – and would in time bear her husband six children: John, David, Susan, Joseph, James and Margaret Ann. Reverend Charles Beatty, Princeton trustee, found her "well-looking, genteel, open; [a] friendly woman."[6] She was John's first instructor until he began attending grammar school at Haddington, and instilled in him a love of the Scriptures that he initially read at the age of four.

The Witherspoons' family pedigree is often ascribed a great deal of his-

---

[3] Joseph Witherspoon, *The History and Genealogy of the Witherspoon Family*, p. 57. City and date of publication unavailable.

[4] Rev. A. Mitchell Hunter, "John Witherspoon in Scotland," *The Witherspoon Bi-Centenary*, p. 581. City and date of publication unavailable.

[5] *Ibid*.

[6] Varnum Lansing Collins, *President Witherspoon* (New York: Arno Press, 1969), Vol. 1, p. 86.

torical weight, and not just because they were a landed family. It is often contended that the source of Witherspoon's love of the Reformed tradition can be found in his mother's relation to John Knox, the early leader of the Scottish Reformation. The orthodox Calvinism that earned him the nickname "Scotch Granite" was in his blood, and he never swayed from his allegiance to the mastermind of the Reformation.[7] One commentator has even given Witherspoon the fitting sobriquet of "John Knox *redivivus*." He would have accepted it warmly.

There was little doubt in John's mind or those of his family where his future was to be found. His theological bent revealed itself early in his life when he was able with little work to recite from memory much of the New Testament and Isaac Watts's *Psalms and Hymns*.[8] By his father's Christian learning and his mother's attentive lessons, Witherspoon was readied, in his own reflective words near the close of life, to "cause the knowledge of God to cover the earth, as the water covers the seas."[9]

Having advanced beyond his grammar school's resources, young Witherspoon moved to the University of Edinburgh at the age of fourteen, where in the next three years he completed his studies for the Masters of Arts. His bracing combination of probity, wit, and religiosity quickly separated him from the crowd. Even the most distinguished aristocratic students would admit respect for his "strong and enlightened understanding."[10] He was well regarded for his "taste in sacred criticism, precision in thinking and a perspicuity of expression rarely attained at so early a period."[11] Here, at Divinity Hall, Witherspoon began to hone the insight and training of which the American Founders would gladly avail themselves.

---

[7] Hunter, p. 582.

[8] John Eidsmoe, *Christianity and the Constitution: The Faith of Our Founding Fathers* (Grand Rapids: Baker House Books), p. 81.

[9] Collins, *op. cit.*, Vol. 1, p. 66.

[10] Joseph Witherspoon, *op. cit.*, p. 57.

[11] "Early American Presbyterian," http://sdsspc1.lsa.umich.edu.presbiow.htm.

An American Leader

A New Map of Scotland According to Gordon of Straloch, 1721. Benton Collection, Division of Maps, Library of Congress.

Paisley

Edinburgh

The Scotland of Witherspoon's upbringing and early ministry.
Birthplace: Yester; Education: Edinburgh; Ministry: Beith and Paisley.

CHURCHMAN AND
THEOLOGICAL POLEMICIST

In keeping with the time-honored profession of his forebears, Witherspoon formally pursued training for the ministry. At the age of twenty-one, after the required two years' probation, he was licensed to preach the gospel. He was presented to the Kirk at Beith by the Earl of Eglington and accepted without opposition in 1745. He would reside there for twelve years. During his time at Beith, Witherspoon was married to Elizabeth Montgomery. Together they would parent ten children, five of whom survived to adulthood.

Witherspoon entered the ministry of the Church of Scotland during a humanist renaissance, a period of new intellectual liberty and literary creativity. At the time, the Church of Scotland was divided between the liberal Moderate party and conservative Popular party. The Moderate party sought to saddle the invigorating spirit of the Enlightenment like their latitudinarian counterparts in the Church of England. As an austere and forthright orthodox Calvinist, Witherspoon was loath to countenance the triumph of this theological temper of moderation. He soon arose as the chief polemicist for orthodox and evangelical Calvinism, "the brainiest man in the Popular party."[12]

Witherspoon saw the moderates as degraders of the apostolic Christian faith. He succinctly captured this liberalizing spirit with which many modern Christians have been at continual odds:

---

[12] Collins, *op. cit.*, Vol. 1, p. 26.

John Witherspoon

In the place of the purity of faith and strictness of morals we have substituted a pliant and fashionable scheme of religion, a fine theory of virtue and morality, a beautiful but unsubstantial idol, raised by human pride, adorned and dressed by human art and supported by the wisdom of words.[13]

When it came to matters of faith, John Witherspoon did not waffle. Whereas moderates sought to reconstruct a Christian edifice built on the unbridled rights of personal conscience, Witherspoon believed the church to be based on unambiguous doctrines that no amount of progress could change. Those principles included the grand truths of the gospel: original sin, Christ's righteousness, justification by free grace, the necessity of regeneration, and the assistance of the Spirit.[14] Man's sole obligation, in his estimation, is "supremely and uniformly to aim at the glory of God."[15] Thus the redoubtable pastor on the perseverance of the saints: "Let no Christian, therefore, give way to desponding thoughts, though infidelity unresisted spread its poison ... though there are few to support the interest of truth and righteousness ... let us not be discouraged. We plead the cause that shall prevail."[16]

John Witherspoon

So moved was Witherspoon by the folly of the Moderate party that he took momentary leave of his usually stern discourse and penned a satirical pamphlet, titled *Ecclesiastical Characteristics*. Among other things, this pungent mockery of theological moderation stated that only those "that are suspected of heresy are to be esteemed men of great genius, vast learning, and uncommon worth. ... [And] when any man is charged with loose

---

[13] *Ibid.*, p. 53.

[14] *Ibid.*, p. 54.

[15] *Ibid.*, p. 45.

[16] *Ibid.*, p. 53.

practices or tendencies to immorality, he is to be screened and protected as much as possible."[17] He pilloried the moderates with stinging accuracy, and his work was a hit with orthodox Calvinists. "The satire that does not bite is good for nothing," he said in his own defense.[18] Contemporary Christians engaged on saving their faith as well as their culture recognize his caricature all too well.

Despite the criticism he received while at Beith, Witherspoon still had the ear of his church, and in 1757 the Laigh Kirk of Paisley sent out a call. Paisley had long been regarded as an urbane hub of opinion and literary activity, a place "where every weaver is a politician."[19] Thus it is to be seen as a mark of the highest approbation and honor that a man insuppressibly orthodox was accepted (though after some haggling) to preside over one of the trendiest parishes in Scotland.

It is often said that Witherspoon dearly loved intelligent argument, and one can only assume that Paisley afforded him ample opportunity. Salvation lay at the focal point of many of his works. His sermon "The Absolute Necessity of Salvation through Christ" admonished his congregation that the gospel was not to be compromised and that at stake was nothing less than the souls of mankind.[20] In response to the Moderate party's charge that he was unconcerned with Christian charity, the never complacent pastor completed an "Inquiry into the Scripture Meaning of Charity" and stated that genuine charity includes "an ardent and unfeigned love for their eternal welfare."[21] Aye, he would say, one indifferent to salvation is no Christian at all.

He continued to author jeremiads on "paganized Christian divines" and general spiritual and moral laxity. The odious effects of moderation on the clergy, morals and popular entertainment rarely escaped his excoriations. Against the buffoonery and immorality of Paisley's popular culture, Witherspoon railed, "[I]s this not taking away the very foundation of morality … and bringing into question the very being of a God?"[22] To the dismay of his Moderate party opponents, Paisley proved to be a center from which Witherspoon's abilities for philosophical, theological and moral suasion would become widely known.

---

[17] *Ibid.*, p. 36.

[18] Hunter, *op. cit.*, p. 582.

[19] Eidsmoe, *op. cit.*, p. 82.

[20] *Ibid.*, p. 82.

[21] *Ibid.*

[22] Collins, *op. cit.*, p. 63.

GOWNSMAN AS GOSPELLER: MISSIONARY TO AMERICA

But in short order, the stage of Scotland would prove to be incapable of supporting Witherspoon's talents and capacities. They were too remarkable to have remained unnoticed for long, and the vigor of his learning, piety and blossoming statesmanship became cramped. His treatises on Justification and Regeneration earned for him wide repute around and outside of Scotland. Witherspoon was soon bombarded with calls from parishes from Dundee and Dublin and Rotterdam, unsuccessful though they were.[23] The reverberation was eventually to be felt in America.

The fledgling College of New Jersey (later Princeton University) was in dire need of leadership. Having lost several of its first five presidents to unexpectedly early deaths, the board of trustees was in search of a man "to give it breadth and flexibility, virility and permanence ... and to gather the real firstfruits."[24] They insisted that he be a confessing orthodox Presbyterian sufficiently endowed with both mental and physical robustness; the customs of the college demanded he be of irreproachable piety and possessed of the broadest scholarship and culture possible.[25] In November of 1766, the Honorable William Peartree Smith, the acting president of the board, wrote and asked Witherspoon to fill the station.

The trustees' act of near-desperation proved to be an unexpected stroke of genius. A commemorative address at Princeton in 1896 by Woodrow Wilson reflected that "it was a piece of providential good

---

[23] Hunter, *op. cit.*, p. 582.

[24] *Ibid.*, p. 70.

[25] Collins, *op. cit.*, p. 71.

DEI SUB NUMINE VIGET

AULA NASSOVICA.

An elevation of Nassau Hall at the College of New Jersey in Princeton, a place Witherspoon grew to love.

fortune that brought such a man to Princeton at such a good time."[26] This compound of statesman and scholar was an appropriate choice for manifold reasons. For one thing, he was liberally educated in what was arguably the finest university in the English-speaking world, and his scholarship had won for him admiration abroad. The aura of British birth and British training still held considerable sway over colonists. Moreover, his education spanned a wide range of disciplines. And as opposed to the narrowness of ministerial training at Oxford or Cambridge, he was interested in the sciences and well-versed in theology, philosophy, philology and literature. In short, he was singularly able to fill any number of academic roles without compromising the caliber of the instruction. Another looming factor in his invitation was that his nationality reflected the burgeoning Scottish immigration at that time. His filling the post would help many other new Scotch-Americans feel at home.

More than anything else, however, the trustees were impressed by

---

[26] Woodrow Wilson, "Princeton in the Nation's Service," a commemorative address delivered at Princeton University on October 21, 1896, printed in the *Memorial Book of the Sesquicentennial Celebration of the Founding of the College of New Jersey and the Ceremonies Inaugurating Princeton University* (New York: Charles Scribner's Sons, 1898), p. 107.

18

John Witherspoon

Witherspoon's position within the Church of Scotland. Primary weight was placed on the ecclesiastical rather than educational influence he might have upon the colonies. The trustees' main concern was "that he would prove a tower of strength in the episcopate controversy through which the Colonies were … passing."[27] At that time, American Presbyterians were embroiled in a controversy between the "New Lights," who placed an emphasis on spiritual rebirth, and the "Old Lights," who were the stalwarts of orthodox doctrine and the steadfastness of Christian life.[28] On the whole, the College had always been aligned with the former, with the latter never allowed any appreciable share of control. But both sides were fully aware that their faction was only contributing to the Anglicans' incipient stronghold on higher education, and it was tacitly understood by more than a few that Witherspoon's acceptance would help mend the rift in the Presbyterian church. The "New Lights" found his fervor for evangelism attractive, while he was acceptable to the "Old Lights" because of his stress on moral Christian living.[29]

A delegation left the college to formally appeal to Witherspoon in 1767. Although his interest was piqued immediately, his wife, Elizabeth, was loath to remove their family from Scotland. Visits, proddings and letters by the likes of Richard Stockton and Dr. Benjamin Rush did very little to dissuade Mrs. Witherspoon from her well-intended obstinacy. The well-being of her children was her constant concern, and she believed that a trans-Atlantic move would disrupt their development. Finally, however, perhaps sensing the gentle

Engraved by R.W. Dodson from a painting by T. Sully. Library of Congress (LC-USZ62-28646).

BENJAMIN RUSH, M.D.

Dr. Benjamin Rush was a Philadelphia physician and one of the trustees of the College of New Jersey. Later, Rush would sign the Declaration of Independence with Witherspoon.

Library of Congress (LC-USZ62 3595).

Richard Stockton was from Princeton, New Jersey, and was a signer of the Declaration of Independence

---

[27] Collins, *op. cit.*, p. 72.

[28] Eidsmoe, *op. cit.*, p. 83.

[29] *Ibid.*

hand of Providence or heeding the urgings of the family's most valued friends, Mrs. Witherspoon acquiesced. The College of New Jersey was ecstatic. The Rev. George Duffield could not hide his jubilance in telling Charles Beatty that "no sooner had did the Letters arrive here from Scotland that Mrs. Witherspoon like another Sarah was willing to follow her husband, than Witherspoon's name dwelt upon every tongue, and the very air of Princeton for Weeks together resounded with nothing but the name of Witherspoon."[30]

GEORGE DUFFIELD DD.

Published by W.P.Farrand N° 170 Market Street Philadelphia

Duffield, of Philadelphia, was a prominent churchman who implored Witherspoon to leave Scotland and assume leadership of the College.

The missionary possibility that lay in front of Witherspoon was the allurement clearly paramount, and he had placed the cause of American Presbyterianism – if not the work of Christ Himself – far in front of the gain of American education.[31] As his biographer Varnum Lansing Collins puts it, "However little others may have thought of it or he himself have realized just then, was the belief that the function of such a college was not merely to educate candidates for the ministry, but also to send out into the widening spheres of colonial life Christian gentlemen and scholarly men of affairs."[32] Indeed, whatever function he might come to discharge, it was the proclamation of Christ that animated Witherspoon, and he was first a minister, bound to the furtherance of God's kingdom. The closing sentences of the humble Scot's first sermon at the College no doubt revealed the cross he understood himself to bear.

I am filled with the greatest concern because it [the college] plainly implies an expectation of duty and service from me, which I fear I shall be ill able to perform. ... Pray that an all sufficient God may give strength from above, and pour down his blessing on the public institution in this place. ... Pray that success may attend the

---

[30] Collins, *op. cit.*, p.89.

[31] *Ibid.*, p. 98.

[32] *Ibid.*, p. 99.

John Witherspoon

Ministry of the gospel in this place. ...[33]

After a taxing voyage of twelve weeks, the doctor had arrived in the colonies aboard the *Peggy* on Sunday, August 7, 1768. In tow were his wife and five children- Ann, the oldest, James, a college student, John, who was eleven, Frances, who had just turned nine, and David, his father's pet and a precocious boy of eight years.[34] A wave of excitement swept over the American colonials who had eagerly awaited his coming. He was lavishly feted and the cause of some competition amongst colonists for the honor of housing him during his rest.

They found in him a stout man with a rigid carriage. Housed beneath unusually bushy eyebrows were alarmingly blue eyes that revealed an alert and active mind. His features were noticeably large, his hair brown and his complexion fair. Flashes of humor and light heartedness seemed invariably to sneak into his speech, in contrast to his grave demeanor. He carried that characteristic the Romans called *gravitas*: "[His] character was stamped in every feature. He had that indefinable quality called presence. ... One listened to him inevitably, confident that here was a man who did not speak save when he had something worth saying."[35]

Transatlantic travel meant one thing: weeks or months crossing the sea on a ship like the Roy, pictured above. Mrs. Witherspoon's anxiety over moving to the New World was probably exacerbated by thoughts of the precarious mode of transport.

Library of Congress (LC-USZ62-60039).

---

[33] *Ibid.*, p.100.

[34] *Ibid.*, p. 103.

[35] *Ibid.*, p. 103.

A map showing Philadelphia and the surrounding area during the colonial period.

John Witherspoon

PRINCETON PHILOSOPHER PRESIDENT AND PROFESSOR

Witherspoon's energy entered the college "like a tonic," invigorating its students and keeping it alive during a time of risk.[36] Officially he served in the capacity of professor of divinity, but in fact he assumed both teaching and administrative duties. The standards of scholarship were at once intensified, the library grew substantially, and a new educational technique called the lecture was introduced. On top of this, Witherspoon scoured the colonies, securing for the college a sizable endowment that would ensure its momentary financial security. The president wasted little time in reconsecrating his college to those great objects its leader saw as fundamental to classic Christian learning.

Witherspoon's conception of the Christian liberal arts is a lodestar guiding its followers to the cultivation of piety, wisdom and prudence. Princeton was conceived, in the words of Woodrow Wilson, as a "school of duty," a place where men would learn of the ancient virtues of the spirit of Christ – the permanent things. As

Library of Congress (LC-USZ62-10463).

Woodrow Wilson (1856-1924), the son of a Presbyterian minister, served as president of Princeton University before becoming governor of New Jersey and later President of the United States.

---

[36] Wilson, *op. cit.*, p. 15.

RES. OF JOHN WITHERSPOON
Mercer Co NJ

In addition to his campus residence, Witherspoon owned a small farm on the outskirts of the village of Princeton. "Tusculum" was a retreat where he pursued gardening as a scientific interest.

Wilson said in eulogizing the aim of Witherspoon's tenure at the college, "It is the business of a university to impart to the rank and file of the men whom it trains the right thought of the world, the thought which it has tested and established, the principles which have stood through the seasons and become at length part of the immemorial wisdom of the race."[37] Both mind and spirit are to be drawn toward the values of classical Christian learning in hope of cultivating those thoughts that realize the duty of righteousness in this world and salvation in the next.[38] Proper education, Witherspoon would agree, is found in mankind's adjustment to God's unchanging law, which affords him a glimpse of truth: "If [education] give them no vision of the true God, it has given them no certain motive to practice the wise lessons they learned."[39] Learning is empty unless it inspires a

---

[37] *Ibid.*, p. 22.

[38] *Ibid.*, p. 20.

[39] *Ibid.*, p. 21.

John Witherspoon

fear and respect of God.

Witherspoon gave breadth and spirit to the college's curriculum. Rather than focusing on specialization, the Presbyterian divine created a training ground for the sons of farmers, politicians and tradesman alike. He had in mind a course of study that would form men's minds for public affairs, church ministry and scholarship. Lectures ranged from eloquence and style of speaking and writing to metaphysics. Lessons on practical statesmanship, the science of government and public duty were also part of college fundamentals. The courses' most notable quality, it was said, was their constant emphasis on accuracy and alertness.

In economics, Witherspoon lectured on the need for hard money instead of paper currency and on the relative advantages of the free market system. Students also were served a hefty dose of social contract theory, emphasizing the need for popular consent of the governed. The subjects of history and French were introduced for the first time. Although he did little true scientific experimentation himself (he liked to think of himself as a "scientific farmer"), Witherspoon was acutely interested in the scientific developments of his day. One of his earliest expenditures at the college was to procure David Rittenhouse's world-famous "Orrery," a complex mechanical model of the solar system and probably the most hailed scientific apparatus in the world.

But no discipline escaped the stabilizing touch of religion and moral philosophy. These were the salt that preserved duty and learning from the decay of time.[40] To Witherspoon, the touchstone of his work was the Christian message. His instructions upon morality to his students could be distilled into his warning, "If sin gives a man no rest, he should give it no quarter."[41] Judeo-Christian morality steadied and lent structure to both coursework and the college as an institution. In Wilson's memorial words, there was "nothing that [gave] such pith to public service as religion."[42] Time and time again Witherspoon struck upon the role that Christian piety must play in education:

> Piety, without literature, is but little profitable; and learning, without piety, is pernicious to others, and ruinous to the possessor. Religion is the grand concern to us all, as we are

---

[40] Wilson, *op. cit.*, p. 21.

[41] Hunter, *op. cit.*, p. 583.

[42] Wilson, *op. cit.*, p. 20.

David Rittenhouse's famous model of the solar system, the "Orrery." Witherspoon purchased the Orrery for the College's students to enhance their education in the natural sciences.

men;–whatever be our calling and profession, the salvation
of our souls is the one thing needful.[43]

This compatibility demanded that education must appeal to the soul,
and the Christian faith to the intellect.

The lectures that Witherspoon gave on moral philosophy – which
included ethics, political science and law – were the first of their kind delivered in an American college.[44]   Because they were circulated among and
used by many a colonist, they were influential outside as well as within the
college. Witherspoon's lectures often were designed to disabuse his students of the "idealistic" philosophy that they had accepted through the
legacy of Congregationalist Jonathan Edwards.   "Idealism" was an
Enlightenment philosophy definitively expounded by Anglican Bishop
George Berkeley, which stated that nothing existed in the world save minds
and ideas. That is, matter is not empirically real; the only realities are the
mind of God and other beings that perceive matter.

The sensible Witherspoon found philosophical idealism repugnant. He
brought with him a new philosophy indigenous to his native land, called
Scottish "common sense philosophy."   Presbyterian ministers Francis
Hutcheson (1694-1746) and Thomas Reid (1710-1796) articulated this new
school of thought, intended as a rejoinder to the skepticism within idealism. It believed that the dictates of common sense – the findings of empir-
ical data from the senses, the moral sense, and practical reason all rolled
into one – were reliable. "This moral sense," maintained Witherspoon in a
Pauline moment, "is precisely the same thing with what, in scripture and
common language, we call conscience. It is the law which our Maker has
written upon our hearts, and both intimates and enforces duty, previous to
all reasoning."[45] Witherspoon was a realist: Practical truths of government
and behavior do not inhere in an abstract object beyond the human realm,
but are to be seen as the fingerprints of God left upon men's hearts and the
norms of Creation. Nature had disclosed God's patterns; it was left for man
to align himself with them.

---

[43] Witherspoon, "Lectures on Divinity," *The Works of the Rev. John Witherspoon* (Philadelphia: William
W. Woodward, 1800-01), Vol. 4, pp. 10-11.

[44] Collins, *op. cit.*, Vol. 2, p. 84.

[45] *An Annotated Edition of Lectures on Moral Philosophy by John Witherspoon*, Jack Scott, ed.
(Newark, Del.: University of Delaware Press, 1982), p. 78.

Library of Congress (LC-USZ62-23059).

Twelve colonies sent delegates to the First Continental Congress, held in Philadelphia's Carpenter's Hall in 1774.

"REAL WHIG" REPUBLICAN PATRIOT

The peculiarities and nuances of the colonies, however, began to leave their mark on "Scotch Granite." The spirit of Americanism quickly crept into his thinking, and he noticed that American solidarity, loyalties and political pragmatism were in some respects uniquely American. Foremost among these eccentricities was the American conception of representative government. Witherspoon's transformation into an American began shortly after he realized that the brewing dispute between the mother country and her colonists was serious. At the beginning of his ministry he had vociferously opposed any attempts of the clergy to deal with politics, but encroachments upon American liberties hit a deep nerve in Witherspoon. The Scottish love of liberty was in his blood, a legacy from John Knox, and the great history of English liberty, from the Magna Carta was ingrained in his mind. The smoking kindling of his love of liberty that began in Scotland was fanned into flame by the arrogance of the British. He knew, along with Edmund Burke, "that to argue the Americans out of their liberties would be to falsify their pedigree."[46] Whatever he might have known about the American mind, this much he knew for sure – that the colonists understood themselves to be entitled to the ancient rights of Englishmen.

On July 21, 1774, Witherspoon finally eschewed his stance on politics and participated in a state convention in New Brunswick intended to make sense of the colonists' plight and set the stage for the soon-to-be-convened Continental Congress. He declared that the Continental Congress was an

---

[46] Wilson, *op. cit.*, p. 23.

authoritative representation of the American people and that their great objects should consist of uniting the colonies to assure their respective safety and assuring Britain that driving the colonists into submission would be either impossible or at the least unprofitable. Among his recommendations to Congress were to "prefer war with all its horrors, and even extermination, to slavery," and to work "until American liberty is settled on a solid basis."[47] The case for freedom had been echoed throughout the colonies for six years; at last he was driven into agreement with it.

SECOND STREET. North from Market St. & CHRIST CHURCH, PHILADELPHIA

A view of Philadelphia's Second Street, north from Market Street.

Christ Church (Anglican/Episcopal) is in center view. Renowned as "the Nation's Church," Christ Church was the parish of many of the founders, including George Washington, Benjamin Franklin, Robert Morris, James Wilson, Dr. Benjamin Rush, Francis Hopkinson and Betsy Ross. Its rectors, Rev. Jacob Duché and Rt. Rev. William White, were chaplains to the Continental Congress.

This change of mind was not rash, for it was attended by deep moral convictions. He now gave an account of himself as "God's minister both in a sacred and civil sense."[48] God had impressed upon him civic responsibility. Biographer Varnum Lansing Collins gave a stirring account of the brooding passion in Witherspoon's soul:

> But like a war-horse scenting the fray, that gentleman could not bear the strain of remaining at Princeton while the Congress of provincial deputies was assembling a scant fifty miles away. Stirring within him was the blood of the ancient spearman. ... [I]t had made him the redoubtable champion of the Popular Party, and it was now calling him to Philadelphia. ...[49]

---

[47] Collins, *op. cit.*, Vol. 1, p. 162.

[48] Hunter, *op. cit.*, p. 583.

[49] Collins, *op. cit.*, Vol. 1, p. 166.

John Witherspoon

Witherspoon's opposition to arbitrary British authority was animated by distinctively Christian theological traditions. The seeds of American liberty were within Christianity's moral framework. The "idea that a people suffering under a tyrant had the right to resist him through their legally constituted representatives was traditional Calvinism."[50] Thus, Protestantism combined with Witherspoon's common sense philosophy to arm pre-Revolutionary America with an evangelical religion aimed at political liberty, order and republican democracy.[51] And it would be this philosophy that helped to beget American independence and constitutionalism.

Whatever may have been spoken privately or penned anonymously, any confusion over Witherspoon's views was abruptly settled on May 17, 1776, when he preached a sermon in Nassau Hall that would be his first political utterance from the pulpit. Titled "The Dominion of Providence over the Passions of Men" (see Appendix A), his salvo was drawn from the tenth verse of the seventy-sixth Psalm and helped propel him to Philadelphia just in time to debate and sign the Declaration of Independence. The sermon was intended as a rallying call to Americans to realize that the time had come for decisive thought and action. Politics had not entered his sermon in response to British ill will, he contended, but instead under the banner of justice, liberty and humanity.

The Dominion of Providence over the Passions of Men.

A

S E R M O N,

PREACHED

At PRINCETON, on the 17th of May, 1776.

BEING

The GENERAL FAST appointed by the Congress through the United Colonies.

To which is added,

An ADDRESS to the Natives of Scotland, residing in America.

BY

JOHN WITHERSPOON, D.D.
President of the College of New-Jersey.

The Second Edition, with Elucidating Remarks.

PHILADELPHIA Printed:
GLASGOW Re-printed;
Sold by the Bookfellers in Town and Country.
MDCCLXXVII.
[Price Six-pence.]

The cover of Witherspoon's most famous sermon, delivered on the eve of American independence. Afterwards, Witherspoon was lauded by Patriots and denounced by Tories.

University Archives. Department of Rare Books and Special Collections. Princeton University Library.

He began by noting that the great distance separating the government of Great Britain from the colonies had made administration imprudent and the misrepresentation of colonial interests inevitable. American interests in liberty, he explained, should be born not out of contempt for legal authority or out of malice, but rather out of the concern for the interests and safety of posterity. In order to conduct the trying affairs of independ-

---

[50] Elmer, *op. cit.*, p. 20.

[51] *Ibid.*

ence with the greatest prudence, Witherspoon recommended attention to religion above all, for "he is the best friend of American liberty who is most sincere and active in promoting true and undefiled religion and who sets himself with the greatest firmness to bear down profanity and immorality of every kind."[52]

The sermon had two primary themes: the duty of resisting tyranny and the necessity of believing that God ultimately brings good out of evil. Disobedience to tyrants was indeed obedience to God, and recourse to arms must always be an appeal to heaven. His exposition was shot through with the Christian maxim that all things, no matter how evil, will eventually work for good for those who love God.

John Witherspoon, the sixth president of the College of New Jersey.

All the disorderly passions of men, whether exposing the innocent to private injury or whether they are the arrows of divine judgment in public calamity, shall in the end be to the praise of God; or, to apply it more particularly to the present state of the American colonies ... the ambition of mistaken princes, the cunning and cruelty of oppressive and corrupt ministers, and even the inhumanity of brutal soldiers ... shall finally promote the glory of God.[53]

The roughly five hundred Presbyterian congregations in America lauded the sermon, and its favorable public reception helped to cement Witherspoon's status as one of the most, if not the most, respected of clergymen in the colonies.

---

[52]Collins, *op. cit.*, Vol. 1, p. 198.

[53] "The Dominion of Providence Over the Passions of Men," *The Selected Writings of John Witherspoon,* Thomas Miller, ed. (Carbondale, Ill.: Southern Illinois University Press, 1990), p. 128.

John Witherspoon

FOUNDING FATHER
PAR EXCELLENCE

Following his elections to the state Revolutionary committees and conventions of New Jersey, the distinguished minister-turned-statesman was sent to the Second Continental Congress in Philadelphia in 1776. Soon after his delegation's arrival, the culmination of days of committee meetings came with the adoption of the "unanimous Declaration of the thirteen United States of America." It was well overdue according to Witherspoon, who believed that the colonies were not only ripe for independence, but "in danger of becoming rotten for the want of it."[54]

During his first year in Congress, Witherspoon was a peregrine politician, ranging from committee to committee, dealing with issues from wagons and clothing to secret correspondence. He affirmed both the Resolution and the Declaration of Independence (and was the only clergyman to sign the latter), took part in the succeeding talks on the Articles of Confederation, was an active figure in forming foreign allegiances, steered the government through bankruptcy, assisted in organizing executive departments to replace inefficient committees, and helped settle the problem of claimed western lands.[55] An avid concern for states' rights buffered his concern for an adequate central government. Added to all this was work in humanitarian areas, including the treatment of prisoners, hospital administration, and the improvement of health and morals generally.[56] He served on more than 120 committees, including three standing committees, two of which – the Board of War and Foreign Affairs – were

---

[54] Ashbel Green, *The Life of the Revd. John Witherspoon*, Henry Lyttleton Savage, ed. (Princeton: Princeton University Press, 1973), pp. 159-60.

[55] Collins, *op. cit.*, Vol. 2, p. 4.

[56] *Ibid*.

The north elevation of the Pennsylvania State House (Independence Hall) in Philadelphia. This building hosted the Second Continental Congress, Confederation Congress and Constitutional Convention.

unparalleled in import. Again, it was his character that called men into agreement: "His strong moral sense ... his resolute courage, his high moral and religious tone were of immense value. ... [H]e was a firm champion," remarked a contemporary.[57]

With regard to the new government, Witherspoon championed the idea of a solid union of colonies. He thus helped to ratify the federal Constitution in 1787 as a member of the New Jersey convention and went on to sign the Articles of Confederation in 1778. He believed that unity among colonies was paramount, and accordingly urged during the Revolution that they "adhere to the interest of the whole body, and that no colony ... make its separate peace, or from the hope of partial distinction, leave others as the victims of ministerial vengeance, but that we ... continue united, and pursue the same measures, till American liberty is settled on a solid basis."[58] It was this hope in the unified destiny of the Confederation that led to such unabashed sanguinity: "Sure I am [that] a well planned

---

[57] *Ibid.*, p. 5.

[58] "Thoughts on American Liberty," *The Works of John Witherspoon*, (Edinburgh: Ogle & Aikman, *et al.*, 1804-5), Vol. 9, pp. 75-76.

John Witherspoon

General George Washington, the victorious commander of the Continental Army, poses beside a field cannon after the Battle of Princeton on January 3, 1777. The College of New Jersey's Nassau Hall is pictured on the horizon.

confederacy among the states of America may hand down the blessings of peace and public order to many generations."[59]   More significant than any abstract formula of efficient government was the moral, social and religious capital – the foundational beliefs – upon which all social structures are built.   Education, civilized community, and piety were the handmaids of religion, and were deemed indispensable for the maintenance of human civilization.   Witherspoon knew full well that "a republic once equally poised must either preserve its virtue or loose its liberty."[60]   He therefore implored his fellow Americans to consecrate their new political order to the great virtues of Christianity in order to build his vision of a "city on a hill":

> Let us endeavour to bring into and keep in credit and repu-
> tation everything that may serve to give vigour to an equal
> republican constitution. Let us cherish a love of piety, order,
> industry, frugality. Let us check every disposition to luxury,
> effeminacy, and the pleasures of a dissipated life. Let us in
> public measures put honour upon modesty and self-denial,
> which is the index of real merit.[61]

Indeed, American nation-building was a moral – if not outright Christian – enterprise. For the Christian political resources of liberty, the rule of law, and republican democracy were, in Witherspoon's mind, what made the Revolutionary period one of extraordinary Christian vision and statesmanship. During his tenure in Congress, he was solicited to draft three religious proclamations on behalf of the national government. These documents (see Appendices B, C and D) demonstrate Witherspoon's conviction that the maintenance of "true religion" is foundational to social and political order.

The affection and respect afforded to him by fellow champions of liberty was superseded in intensity only by hatred for him among British loyalists. If there is no better witness to a patriot's status than the amount of venom spouted by his enemies, then Witherspoon should be ranked as a Founder *par excellence*. The British went so far as to hang and burn an effigy of him, and, tragically, a man bearing a likeness to Witherspoon was misidentified by British troops and killed. No less a figure than Dr. Adam Ferguson, professor of moral philosophy at Edinburgh University and a

---

[59] "Speech in Congress Upon the Confederation," *ibid.*, Vol. 9, p. 140.

[60] "Sermon Delivered at a Public Thanksgiving after Peace," *ibid.*, Vol. 5, p. 266.

[61] *Ibid.*, pp. 269-70.

trenchant opponent to independence, wrote a letter bemoaning the seditious doctor:

> We have 1200 miles of territory occupied by about 300,000 people of which there are about 150,000 with Johnny Witherspoon at their head. ... I am not sure that if proper measures were taken but we should reduce Johnny Witherspoon to the small support of Franklin [and] Adams ... but I tremble at the thought of their cunning and determination opposed to us.[62]

Witherspoon, always stoic, would have been quietly flattered.

The idea that Witherspoon secretly led a junta of American elites was a widespread myth. A British officer writing to Sir Guy Carleton fingered Witherspoon as that "political firebrand who perhaps had not a less share in the Revolution than Washington himself. He poisons the minds of his young students and through them the continent."[63] A satirical poem written by Rev. Dr. Odell, an Anglican minister of Burlington, also revealed the height to which Tory concern over the formidable doctor had risen. He was as "fierce as the fiercest, foremost of the first," it moaned. In closing it offered that "dog" who claimed "sound religion" to what Odell hoped would be the unforgiving judgment of heaven. It was a most scathing sally indeed, but it reflected the extent to which the American cause was inextricably linked to the undaunted Christian politics of Witherspoon.

As the American Revolution pressed on, Princeton became a crucible for revolutionary politics. Since September 1776, American troops had been stationed at Princeton. Along with their proximity to the state legislature, the distraction of the soldiery and military traffic proved too alluring to most of the students.[64] It is not altogether surprising then that they took literally the president's oft-quoted dictum that "when liberty, prosperity, and life are at stake, we must not think of being scholars but soldiers." A group of volunteers formed amongst the undergraduate body and proceeded to enlist.[65] The clamor of war reached such a fevered pitch that Witherspoon had no choice other than to dismiss the college. This turned out to be fortunate when on December 7, 1776, the British took quarter in the empty college buildings, homes and churches. The British transformed

---

[62] Collins, *op. cit.*, Vol. 2, p. 35.

[63] Green, *op. cit.*, p. 2.

[64] Collins, *op. cit.*, Vol. 2, p. 88.

[65] *Ibid.*, p. 90.

Nassau Hall into barracks and stables, plundering furniture, apparel and even the college's precious collection of books and writings. The battle of Princeton reached its climax just south of Nassau Hall, with General Washington's broken army storming the college campus. Even today Princeton's buildings bear the effect of Revolutionary troops' artillery.

Hoping for the best, Witherspoon duly announced that the college had been reopened and summoned his students to reconvene at Princeton on July 8, 1777. The school struggled to stay alive despite the dearth of adequate structures, finances and academic resources. For months, its president labored to secure money from the government and private donors to breathe life into a worn school.

The Pennsylvania Evening Post, Thursday, June 26, 1777, p. 1. The Historical Society of Pennsylvania (HSP).

Witherspoon published a notice in The Pennsylvania Evening Post announcing the resumption of classes on July 8, 1777. Following General Washington's victory at the Battle of Princeton, the British army left the campus in utter disarray, and Witherspoon labored for years to rebuild the college.

Philadelphia, June 24, 1777.

THE Undergraduates of the College of New-Jersey are desired to repair to Princeton without delay, as College orders will begin on Tuesday, the 8th day of next month. They are desired to take all possible pains, to provide themselves with books, according to their standing and future studies, which are already known to them. It is hoped, that all of them have been pursuing their studies separately as well as their circumstances would allow, and that they will now apply with extraordinary diligence, to recover the ground that has been necessarily lost. The seniors in particular are requested to come prepared for continuing at Princeton until the end of September, as the examination for Batchelor's degrees will not be this year as formerly, in the middle of August, but immediately before commencement.
JOHN WITHERSPOON.

N. B. The printers of newspapers in this and the adjacent states are requested to insert the above, for the information of those concerned.

John Witherspoon

PRESBYTERIAN PATRIARCH

At the close of the Revolutionary War, Witherspoon was sixty years old. The peace forged between the warring parties brought to an end six years of unbearable strain for him and his family (having lost family members in the effort). He continued to be adorned with recognition and distinction, but his worn body, coupled with financial problems, made him ill at ease in his final days. Nonetheless, as a sort of Revolutionary celebrity, he sailed to Europe, where he preached and canvassed the well-to-do for donations for the college. Of his three great roles, that of hands-on statesman was virtually finished, his membership in the Continental Congress having ended in 1782.[66] As a clergyman, however, Witherspoon's career would now reach its apex, as he took upon himself the crucial role in the first meeting of the General Assembly of the Presbyterian Church of the United States of America.

HIGH STREET, with the First Presbyterian CHURCH, PHILADELPHIA

Philadelphia was the third largest English-speaking city in the world, with 40,000 inhabitants. It soon became a hub for revolutionary activity, hosting the First and Second Continental Congresses and later governments of the United States of America.

High Street with the First Presbyterian Church in Philadelphia. Library of Congress (LC-USZ262-3238).

---

[66] Hunter, *op. cit.*, p. 585.

THE SECOND PRESBYTERIAN CHURCH,

Northwest corner of Third and Mulberry (Arch) streets.

FINISHED A. D. 1752.   STEEPLE COMPLETED 1763-'64.

Witherspoon moderated the first General Assembly of the Presbyterian Church of the United States of America. Second Presbyterian Church in Philadelphia hosted the historic meeting in May, 1789. Concurrent with Presbyterian polity deliberations, a great national debate over ratification of the United States Constitution ensued.

By 1785, it had become painfully clear that Witherspoon's church had outgrown its original colonial organization. The respected Presbyterian patriarch was appointed to head a committee on discipline and government that would compile a system of general rules and procedures for each new synod. At stake was nothing less than the future of the Presbyterian Church in America.

The gathering of the first General Assembly was the crowning point of Witherspoon's ministerial career. From this gathering, Presbyterians gained a confession, catechisms, a directory of worship, and a "System of General Rules" for church administration. As always, Witherspoon's vision of Presbyterian unity never came at the expense of either doctrinal orthodoxy or religious liberty. By virtue of his position as moderator, he became the most distinguished American clergyman of the moment.

The historic adoption of the Church's constitution, which ensured the vitality of one of the nation's strongest institutions, was all the more important when one remembers that the Constitutional Convention of the United States met only four blocks away. Witherspoon had opted to impress his mark upon the future of American Christianity, though he might possibly have attended the Convention. The new organization of the church reflected his ideals in the same way that the American Constitution did, for they were both the "fruit of the same great national impulse of the time to give the social life its complete expression by a policy of national dimension and spirit."[67]

---

[67] Collins, *op. cit.*, Vol. 2., p. 161.

John Witherspoon

PREFACE.

THE Synod of New-York and Philadelphia, *being about to establish a system of union and form of discipline for themselves and the subordinate bodies under their care, thought it proper to begin with laying down a few general principles by which they have been governed in deciding upon the several parts of the plan. This, they hope, will make the whole better understood, as well as prevent, in some degree, such rash and uncandid reflections as commonly proceed from an imperfect view of any subject.*

The Synod are unanimously of opinion,

I. That ' God alone is Lord of the conscience, ' and hath left it free from the doctrines and ' commandments of men, which are in any thing ' contrary to his word; or beside it in matters of ' faith or worship.' Therefore they consider the rights of private judgment in all matters that regard religion as universal and unalienable. They do not even wish to see any religious constitution aided by the civil power, further than may be necessary for protection and security, and at the same time may be equal and common to all others.

II. That in perfect consistency with the above principle of common right, every Christian church, or union and association of particular churches, is entitled to declare the terms of admission into it, and the qualifications of its ministers and members, as well as the whole system of its internal government, which Christ has appointed

The Preface to a system of general rules and procedures for the Presbyterian Synods of New York and Philadelphia. Witherspoon headed the committee that drafted this document, thus laying the foundation for the first General Assembly of the Presbyterian Church of the United States.

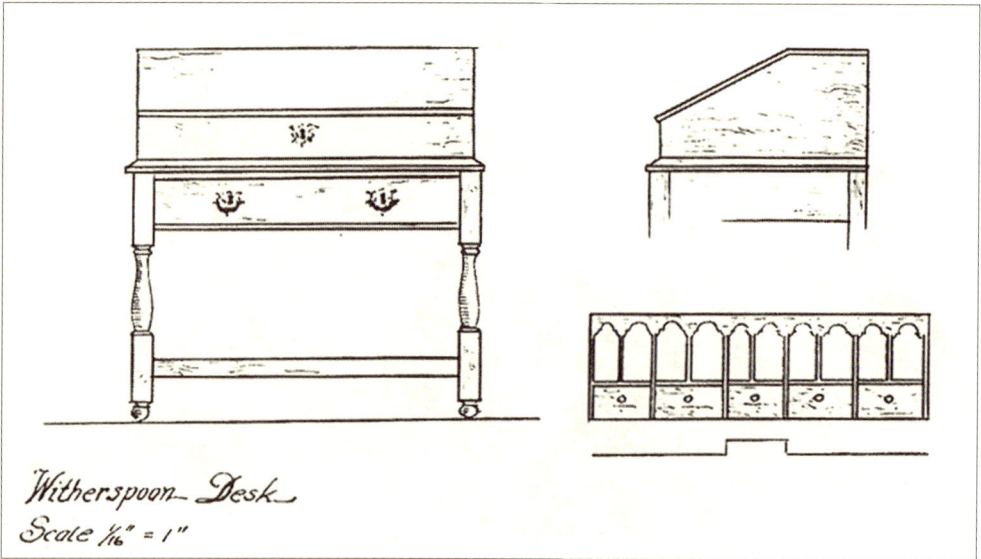

Witherspoon Desk
Scale ⅟₁₆" = 1"

The desk Witherspoon used for writing his lectures and sermons.

WITHERSPOON'S LEGACY: A LEGION OF LEADERS

It was this "great national impulse" that was the priceless legacy of Witherspoon. For this man of "extraordinary force, versatility and charm" stirred the imaginations of generations of America's foremost historical figures in a way few others did.[68] That this "national impulse" inspired his contemporaries is undeniable. Even more important than his own works were the legion of leaders whom he inspired – the general public who devoured his writings, the scores of politicians and clergymen who heard his speeches, and the multitudes of students who eagerly sought his wisdom. Witherspoon's most distinguished contribution is the lives of those who carried his message.

One need look no further to corroborate this than at the caliber of students the doctor instructed. The number of men mentored by him who went on to the most respected posts in education and politics is simply staggering. In understanding the profound influence of Witherspoon,

Engraving of Arch Street with Second Presbyterian Church Independence National Historical Park.

West Prospect of Philadelphia's Arch Street, with the prominent spire of Second Presbyterian Church in the center.

---

[68] *Ibid.*, p. 182.

one should keep in mind that the college really was a seminary, intent on producing men of Christian ambitions and callings and with the spirit of Christian piety permeating its dynamics. Thus it is nothing short of remarkable that Witherspoon's seminary served not only as a primary source of new ministers, but also as a center of civil learning and public service.[69] Chief among the graduates of the college during his presidency were a U.S. vice president (Aaron Burr); twelve members of the Continental Congress; five delegates to the Constitutional Convention; forty-nine U.S. representatives; twenty-eight U.S. senators; three Supreme Court justices; eight U.S. district judges; one secretary of state; three attorneys general; and two foreign ministers. Moreover, besides these national office-holders, twenty-six graduates were state judges, seventeen served in state constitutional conventions, and fourteen were members of state conventions that ratified the federal Constitution.[70] Added to this were 114 ministers, nineteen of whom became presidents of or professors at educational institutions ranging from New York to Georgia.

Aaron Burr, Jr., the grandson of Rev. Jonathan Edwards, was arguably Witherspoon's most infamous student. He mortally wounded Alexander Hamilton in a duel at Weehawken, New Jersey, on July 11, 1804.

However, most prominent among Witherspoon's students was future President James Madison. So delighted was the Virginian by his time with the doctor that, following his graduation in 1771, he stayed an extra year to study Hebrew while possibly toying with the idea of entering the ministry.[71] Witherspoon's impact on Madison can be gauged by the fact that the very principles with which Madison's thought informed the Constitution are nearly identical to many of the philosophies inculcated by his teacher. Most notably, the Christian doctrine of the depravity of man, a touchstone of Calvinist theology, finds eloquent expression by Madison's pen in *The Federalist*. Indeed, both Witherspoon and Madison were acutely conscious of man's inclination toward vice. Witherspoon therefore favored government restraints to prevent the wicked from growing oppressive and tyrannical. From this idea came the concept of separation of powers and a sys-

---

[69] Elmer, *op. cit.*, p. 14.

[70] James McLachlan, *et al.*, eds., *Princetonians: A Biographical Dictionary* (Princeton: Princeton University Press, 1976-91).

[71] John Murrin, "Religion and Politics in America from the First Settlement to the Civil War," *Religion and American Politics: From the Colonial Period to the 1980s*, Mark Noll, ed. (New York: Oxford University Press, 1990), pp. 41-42n.

John Witherspoon

A young James Madison, future father of the Constitution and President of the United States. Madison was Witherspoon's most famous pupil.

tem of checks and balances, which Witherspoon passed on to the "Father of the Constitution." In the estimation of at least one historian, Witherspoon's introduction of these concepts to American government through Madison is his most unique contribution to history.[72]

As his days drew to a close, Witherspoon fought bouts of dizziness, insomnia and poor vision bordering on blindness. Ever composed, he said that if it was God's pleasure to take his eyesight and nerves, then it was of little concern to him. During the last two years of his life, his third cousin, John Ramsay Witherspoon, was employed as the doctor's private secretary. John Ramsay wrote of Witherspoon's death in 1794, "Dr. Witherspoon's manner at that moment had combined the simplicity of a child, the humility of a patriarch, and the dignity of a prince."[73]

---

[72] Eidsmoe, *op. cit.*, p. 89.

[73] Collins, *op. cit.*, Vol. 2, p. 234.

John Witherspoon

THE LEAVEN OF JOHN WITHERSPOON'S LIFE

In his work *Christianity and the Constitution: The Faith of Our Founding Fathers*, John Eidsmoe has distilled the legacy of Witherspoon's life and works into a number of principles. It would serve our purposes well to summarily recount his statement of these:

1. An unequivocal belief in the Providence of God and the destiny of man. As opposed to the Enlightenment thinkers many historians are wont to credit with the American Founding, Witherspoon firmly believed in God's personal intervention in the affairs of men and history, directing both towards their ultimate fulfillment in Christ's rule. The American order, in his mind, was a product of Providence.

2. A recognition of the doctrine of original sin. Again, Witherspoon departed from the Enlightenment's fascination with unlimited human progress, in asserting that "nothing is more plain from [S]cripture, or better supported by daily experience, than that man by nature is in fact incapable of recovery without the power of God specially interposed."[74] While holding to the doctrine of total depravity, Witherspoon still conceived of man as a moral agent, with religious and civic responsibilities. Thus, at the same time as he recognized the need for human redemption, he was able to call upon the natural law written on the hearts of men as the judge of every man's conscience.

3. The declaration of salvation only through Christ, which beckoned him to proclaim that "Religion is the grand concern of us all. ... [T]he sal-

---

[74] Eidsmoe, *op. cit.*, p. 88.

Witherspoon, a leader in spiritual, intellectual and political matters, was well-suited to help shape a nascent republic.

vation of our souls is the one thing needful."[75] Witherspoon's mission was a Christian one – to save souls in the name of Christ.

4. The necessity of liberty, be it personal, political, or religious. Witherspoon held the traditional Calvinist view that government that exceeds its authority is not legitimate. He maintained that Christianity called upon its believers "to defend and secure rights of conscience in the most equal and impartial manner."[76] As a defender of limited government, he believed in natural rights, including that of property.

5. A hope in an America blessed by God and working to his glory. He did not necessarily envisage what one might call a New Israel, but his opinion undoubtedly was that American society and government should be founded upon the great political ideals of Christianity: the brotherhood and equality of all men, the humane rule of law, the common good of the society, and the absolute necessity of religion in sustaining both liberty and civilized community.

These were Witherspoon's fundamental beliefs. And for this reason it has been said of him, "John Adams called him a son of liberty. So he was. But first, he was a son of the Cross."[77]

Perhaps never in American history had a situation so pregnant with possibilities found a man so able to take upon himself its manifold burdens. In his biographer's words, for once "a man of extraordinary force, versatility, and charm had found the place exactly suited to give full swing and scope to every element of power within him. He seems to have come at the right moment, to the right spot, in the right way."[78]

His political work aside, Witherspoon was first and foremost a man of duty and service, a clergyman and an educator. He was faithful to these tasks in the hope that he "might be instrumental in furnishing the minds, and improving the talents, of those who might hereafter be the ministers of

---

[75] *Ibid.*, p. 89.

[76] *Ibid.*, p. 90.

[77] *Ibid.*, p. 92

[78] Collins, *op. cit.*, Vol. 2, p. 182.

John Witherspoon

the everlasting gospel."[79]   The leaven of Witherspoon still works in the minds and souls of those who seek to emulate his courage and sagacity.   It is a legacy above all of piety, a belief in purpose and truth.   Indeed, in commemorating Witherspoon, Woodrow Wilson cautions his followers, in the words of the 90th Psalm, "So teach us to number our days, that we may apply our hearts unto wisdom."[80]

Matthew F. Rose is a graduate (Class of 1999) of Wabash College in Crawfordsville, Indiana, and a native of Medina, North Dakota. During the summer of 1998, he was a Witherspoon Fellow at the Family Research Council in Washington, D.C.

[79] *Ibid.*, p. 197.

[80] Wilson, *op. cit.*, p. 20.

The Dominion of Providence over the Passions of Men.

A

S E R M O N,

PREACHED

AT PRINCETON, on the 17th of MAY, 1776.

BEING

The GENERAL FAST appointed by the
CONGRESS through the UNITED COLONIES.

TO WHICH IS ADDED,

An ADDRESS to the NATIVES of SCOTLAND,
reſiding in AMERICA.

BY

JOHN WITHERSPOON, D.D.

Preſident of the College of NEW-JERSEY.

The Second EDITION, with Elucidating REMARKS.

PHILADELPHIA PRINTED:
GLASGOW RE-PRINTED;
Sold by the Bookſellers in Town and Country.

MDCCLXXVII.

[PRICE SIX-PENCE.]

*The cover of Witherspoon's most famous sermon, delivered on the eve of
American independence. Afterwards, Witherspoon was lauded by
Patriots and denounced by Tories.*

APPENDIX A

THE DOMINION OF PROVIDENCE OVER THE PASSIONS OF MEN

A sermon preached at Princeton on the 17th of May 1776. Being the General Fast appointed by the Congress through the United Colonies. Dedicated to the Hon. John Hancock Esq. President of the Congress of the United States of America. To which is added an Address to the natives of Scotland residing in America.

PSALM lxxvi. 10.
Surely the wrath of Man shall praise thee; the remainder of Wrath shalt thou restrain.

There is not a greater evidence either of the reality or the power of religion, than a firm belief of God's universal presence, and a constant attention to the influence and operation of his providence. It is by this means that the Christian may be said, in the emphatical scripture language, "to walk with God, and to endure as seeing him who is invisible."

The doctrine of divine providence is very full and complete in the sacred oracles. It extends not only to things which we may think of great moment, and therefore worthy of notice, but to things the most indifferent and inconsiderable; "Are not two sparrows sold for a farthing," says our Lord, "and one of them falleth not to the ground without your heavenly Father";

nay, "the very hairs of your head are all numbered.["] It extends not only to things beneficial and salutary, or to the direction and assistance of those who are the servants of the living God; but to things seemingly most hurtful and destructive, and to persons the most refractory and disobedient. He overrules all his creatures, and all their actions. Thus we are told, that "fire, hail, snow, vapour, and stormy wind, fulfil his word," in the course of nature; and even to the most impetuous and disorderly passions of men, that are under no restraint from themselves, are yet perfectly subject to the dominion of Jehovah. They carry his commission, they obey his orders, they are limited and restrained by his authority, and they conspire with every thing else in promoting his glory. There is the greater need to take notice of this, that men are not generally sufficiently aware of the distinction between the law of God and his purpose; they are apt to suppose, that as the temper of the sinner is contrary to the one, so the outrages of the other are able to defeat the other; than which nothing can be more false. The truth is plainly asserted, and nobly expressed by the Psalmist in the text, "Surely the wrath of man shall praise thee; the remainder of wrath shalt thou restrain."

This psalm was evidently composed as a song of praise for some signal victory obtained, which was at the same time a remarkable deliverance from threatening danger.   The author was one or other of the later prophets, and the occasion probably the unsuccessful assault of Jerusalem, by the army of Sennacherib king of Assyria, in the days of Hezekiah. Great was the insolence and boasting of his generals and servants against the city of the living God, as may be seen in the thirty-sixth chapter of Isaiah. Yet it pleased God to destroy their enemies, and, by his own immediate interposition, to grant them deliverance. Therefore the Psalmist says in the fifth and sixth verses of this psalm, "The stout-hearted are spoiled, they have slept their sleep. None of the men of might have found their hands. At thy rebuke, O God of Jacob! both the chariot and the horse are cast into a deep sleep." After a few more remarks to the same purpose, he draws the inference, or makes the reflection in the text, "Surely the wrath of man shall praise thee; the remainder of wrath shalt thou restrain["]: which may be paraphrased thus, The fury and injustice of oppressors shall bring in a tribute of praise to thee; the influence of thy righteous providence shall be clearly discerned; the countenance and support thou wilt give to thine own people shall be gloriously illustrated; thou shalt set the bounds which the

penetrate. It is the duty of every good man to place the most unlimited confidence in divine wisdom, and to believe that those measures of providence that are most unintelligible to him, are yet planned with the same skill, and directed to the same great purposes as others, the reason and tendency of which he can explain in the clearest manner. But where revelation and experience enables us to discover the wisdom, equity, or mercy of divine providence, nothing can be more delightful or profitable to a serious mind, and therefore I beg your attention to the following remarks.

In the first place, the wrath of man praises God, as it is an example and illustration of divine truth, and clearly points out the corruption of our nature, which is the foundation stone of the doctrine of redemption. Nothing can be more absolutely necessary to true religion, than a clear and full conviction of the sinfulness of our nature and state. Without this there can be neither repentance in the sinner, nor humility in the believer. Without this all that is said in scripture of the wisdom and mercy of God in providing a Saviour, is without force and without meaning. Justly does our Saviour say, "The whole have no need of a physician, but those that are sick. I came not to call the righteous, but sinners to repentance." Those who are not sensible that they are sinners, will treat every exhortation to repentance, and every offer of mercy, with disdain or defiance.

But where can we have a more affecting view of the corruption of our nature, than in the wrath of man, when exerting itself in oppression, cruelty, and blood? It must be owned, indeed, that this truth is abundantly manifest in times of great tranquility. Others may, if they please, treat the corruption of our nature as a chimera: for my part, I see it every where, and I feel it every day. All the disorders in human society, and the greatest part even of the unhappiness we are exposed to, arises from the envy, malice, covetousness, and other lusts of man. If we and all about us were just what we ought to be in all respects, we should not need to go any further for heaven, for it would be upon earth. But war and violence present a spectacle, still more awful. How affecting is it to think, that the lust of domination should be so violent and universal? That men should so rarely be satisfied with their own possessions and acquisitions, or even with the benefit that would arise from mutual service, but should look upon the happiness and tranquility of others, as an obstruction to their own? That, as if the great law of nature, were not enough, "Dust thou art, and to dust thou shalt return," they should be so furiously set for the destruction of each other?

It is shocking to think, since the first murder of Abel by his brother Cain, what havoc has been made of man by man in every age. What is it that fills the pages of history, but the wars and contentions of princes and empires? What vast numbers has lawless ambition brought into the field, and delivered as a prey to the destructive sword?

If we dwell a little upon the circumstances, they become deeply affecting. The mother bears a child with pain, rears him with the laborious attendance of many years; yet in the prime of life, in the vigor of health, and bloom of beauty, in a moment he is cut down by the dreadful instruments of death. "Every battle of the warrior is with a confused noise, and garments rolled in blood"; but the horror of the scene is not confined to the field of slaughter. Few go there unrelated, or fall unlamented; in every hostile encounter, what must be the impression upon the relations of the deceased? The bodies of the dead can only be seen, or the cries of the dying heard for a single day, but many days shall not put an end to the mourning of a parent for a beloved son, the joy and support of his age, or of the widow and helpless offspring, for a father taken away in the fullness of health and vigor.

But if this may be justly said of all wars between man and man, what shall we be able to say that is suitable to the abhorred scene of civil war between citizen and citizen? How deeply affecting is it, that those who are the same in complexion, the same in blood, in language, and in religion, should, notwithstanding, butcher one another with unrelenting rage, and glory in the deed? That men should lay waste the fields of their fellow subjects, with whose provision they themselves had been often fed, and consume with devouring fire those houses in which they had often found a hospitable shelter.

These things are apt to overcome a weak mind with fear, or overwhelm it with sorrow, and in the greatest number are apt to excite the highest indignation, and kindle up a spirit of revenge. If this last has no other tendency than to direct and invigorate the measure of self-defense, I do not take upon me to blame it, on the contrary, I call it necessary and laudable.

But what I mean at this time to prove by the preceding reflections, and wish to impress on your minds, is the depravity of our nature. James iv. 1. "From whence come wars and fighting among you? come they not hence even from your lusts that war in your members?" Men of lax and corrupt principles, take great delight in speaking to the praise of human nature, and extolling its dignity without distinguishing what it was, at its first creation, from what it is in its present fallen state. These fine speculations are very grateful to a worldly mind. They are also much more pernicious to uncautious and unthinking youth, than even the temptations to a dissolute and sensual life, against which they are fortified by the dictates of natural conscience, and a sense of public shame. But I appeal from these visionary reasonings to the history of all ages, and the inflexible testimony of daily experience. These will tell us what men have been in their practice, and from thence you may judge what they are by nature, while unrenewed. If I am not mistaken, a cool and candid attention, either to the past history, or present state of the world, but above all, to the ravages of lawless power, ought to humble us in the dust. It should at once lead us to acknowledge the just view given us in scripture of our lost state; to desire the happy influence of renewing grace each for ourselves; and to long for the dominion of righteousness and peace, when "men shall beat their swords into plow-shares, and their spears into pruning hooks; when nation shall not lift up sword against nation, neither shall they learn war any more." * Mic. iv. 3.

2. The wrath of man praiseth God, as it is the instrument in his hand for bringing sinners to repentance, and for the correction and improvement of his own children. Whatever be the nature of the affliction with which he visits either persons, families, or nations; whatever be the disposition or intention of those whose malice he employs as a scourge; the design on his

---

*I cannot help embracing this opportunity of making a remark or two upon a virulent reflection thrown out against this doctrine, in a well known pamphlet, *Common Sense*. The author of that work impresses himself thus: "If the first king of any country was by election, that likewise establishes a precedent for the next; for to say, that the right of all future generations is taken away, by the act of the first electors, in their choice not only of a king, but of a family of kings forever, hath no parallel in or out of scripture, but the doctrine of original sin, which supposes the free will of all men lost in Adam; and from such comparison, and it will admit of no other, hereditary succession can derive no glory. For in Adam all sinned, and as in the first electors all obeyed: as in the one all mankind were subjected to Satan, and in the other to sovereignty; as our innocence was lost in the first, and our authority in the last; and as both disable us from re-assuming some former state and privilege, it unanswerably follows that original sin and hereditary succession are parallels. Dishonorable rank! Inglorious connexion! Yet the most subtle sophist cannot produce a juster simile."† Without the shadow of reasoning, he is pleased to represent the doctrine of original sin as an object of contempt or abhorrence. I beg leave to demur a little to the candor, the prudence, and the justice of this proceeding.

1. Was it modest or candid for a person without name or character, to talk in this supercilious manner of a doctrine that has been espoused and defended by many of the greatest and best men that the world ever saw, and makes an essential part of the established creeds and confessions of all the Protestant churches without exception? I thought the grand modern plea had been freedom of sentiment, and charitable thoughts of one another. Are so many of us, then, beyond the reach of this

part is, to rebuke men for iniquity, to bring them to repentance, and to promote their holiness and peace. The salutary nature and sanctifying influence of affliction in general, is often taken notice of in scripture, both as making a part of the purpose of God, and the experience of his saints. Heb. xii. 11. "Now, no affliction for the present seemeth to be joyous, but grievous: Nevertheless, afterwards it yieldeth the peaceable fruit of righteousness unto them which are exercised thereby." But what we are particularly led to observe by the subject of this discourse is, that the wrath of man, or the violence of the oppressor that praiseth God in this respect, it has a peculiar tendency to alarm the secure conscience, to convince and humble the obstinate sinner. This is plain from the nature of the thing, and from the testimony of experience. Public calamities, particularly the destroying sword, is so awful that it cannot but have a powerful influence in leading men to consider the presence and the power of God. It threatens them not only in themselves, but touches them in all that is dear to them, whether relations or possessions. The Prophet Isaiah says, Is. xxvi. 8, 9. "Yea, in the way of thy judgments, O Lord, have we waited for thee, – for when thy judgments are in the earth, the inhabitants of the world will learn righteousness." He considers it as the most powerful mean of alarming the secure and subduing the obstinate. Is xxvi. 11. "Lord when thy hand is lifted up, they will not see, but they shall see and be ashamed for their envy at the people, yea the fire of thine enemies shall devour them." It is also sometimes represented as a symptom of a hopeless and irrevocable state, when public judgments have no effect. Thus says the prophet

gentleman's charity? I do assure him that such presumption and self-confidence are no recommendation to me, either of his character or sentiments.

2. Was it prudent, when he was pleading a public cause, to speak in such approbious terms of a doctrine, which he knew, or ought to have known, was believed and professed by, I suppose, a great majority of very different denominations. Is this gentleman ignorant of human nature, as well as an enemy to the Christian faith? Are men so little tenacious of their religious sentiments, whether true or false? The prophet thought otherwise, who said, *Hath a nation changed their gods which yet are no gods?* Was it the way to obtain the favor of the public, to despise what they hold sacred? Or shall we suppose this author so astonishingly ignorant, as to think that all men now, whose favor is worth asking, have given up the doctrine of the New Testament? If he does, he is greatly mistaken.

3. In fine, I ask, where was the justice of this proceeding? Is there so little to be said for the doctrine of original sin, that it is not to be refuted, but despised? Is the state of the world such, as to render this doctrine not only false, but incredible? Has the fruit been of such a quality as to exclude all doubts of the goodness of the tree? On the contrary, I cannot help being of opinion, that such has been the visible state of the world in every age, as cannot be accounted for on any other principles than what we learn from the word of God, that *the imagination of the heart of man is only evil from his youth, and that continually.* Gen. vi. 5.- viii. 21.

†*Common Sense, page 11. Bradford's Edition.*

John Witherspoon

Jeremiah, Jer. v. 3. "O Lord, are not thine eyes upon the truth? thou hast stricken them, but they have not grieved; thou hast consumed them, but they have refused to receive correction: they have made their faces harder than a rock, they have refused to return." We can easily see in the history of the children of Israel, how severe strokes brought them to submission and penitence, Ps. lxxviii. 34, 35. "When he slew them, then they sought him, and they returned and inquired early after God, and they remembered that God was their rock, and the high God their redeemer."

Both nations in general, and private persons, are apt to grow remiss and lax in a time of prosperity and seeming security; but when their earthly comforts are endangered or withdrawn, it lays them under a kind of necessity to seek for something better in their place. Men must have comfort from one quarter or another. When earthly things are in a pleasing and promising condition, too many are apt to find their rest, and be satisfied with them as their only portion. But when the vanity and passing nature of all created comfort is discovered, they are compelled to look for something more durable as well as valuable. What therefore, can be more to the praise of God, than that when a whole people have forgotten their resting place, when they have abused their privileges, and despised their mercies, they should by distress and suffering be made to hearken to the rod, and return to their duty?

There is an inexpressible depth and variety in the judgments of God, as in all his other works; but we may lay down this as a certain principle, that if there were no sin, there could be no suffering. Therefore they are certainly for the correction of sin, or for the trial, illustration, and perfecting of the grace and virtue of his own people. We are not to suppose, that those who suffer most, or who suffer soonest, are therefore more criminal than others. Our Saviour himself thought it necessary to give a caution against this rash conclusion, as we are informed by the evangelist Luke, Luke xiii. 1. "There were present at that season some that told him of the Galileans, whose blood Pilate had mingled with their sacrifices. And Jesus answering said unto them, Suppose ye that these Galileans were sinners above all the Galileans, because they suffered such things? I tell you nay, but except ye repent, ye shall all likewise perish." I suppose we may say with sufficient warrant, that it often happens, that those for whom God hath designs of the greatest mercy, are first brought to the trial, that they may enjoy in due time the salutary effect of the unpalatable medicine.

I must also take leave to observe, and I hope no pious humble sufferer will be unwilling to make the application, that there is often a discernable mixture of sovereignty and righteousness in providential dispensations. It is the prerogative of God to do what he will with his own, but he often displays his justice itself, by throwing into the furnace those, who though they may not be visibly worse than others, may yet have more to answer for, as having been favored with more distinguished privileges, both civil and sacred. It is impossible for us to make a just and full comparison of the character either of persons or nations, and it would be extremely foolish for any to attempt it, either for increasing their own security, or impeaching the justice of the Supreme Ruler. Let us therefore neither forget the truth, nor go beyond it. "His mercy fills the earth." He is also "known by the judgment which he executeth." The wrath of man in its most tempestuous rage, fulfills his will, and finally promotes the good of his chosen.

3. The wrath of man praiseth God, as he sets bounds to it, or restrains it by his providence, and sometimes makes it evidently a mean of promoting and illustrating his glory.

There is no part of divine providence in which a greater beauty and majesty appears, than when the Almighty Ruler turns the counsels of wicked men into confusion, and makes them militate against themselves. If the psalmist may be thought to have had a view in this text to the truths illustrated in the two former observations, there is no doubt at all that he had a particular view to this, as he says in the latter part of the verse, "the remainder of wrath shalt thou restrain." The scripture abounds with instances, in which the designs of oppressors were either wholly disappointed, or in execution fell far short of the malice of their intention, and in some they turned out to the honor and happiness of the persons or the people, whom they were intended to destroy. We have an instance of the first of these in the history to which my text relates.* We have also an instance in Esther, in which the most mischievous designs of Haman, the son of Hammedatha the Agagite against Mordecai the Jew, and the nation from which he sprung, turned out at last to his own destruction, the honor of Mordecai, and the salvation and peace of his people.

From the New Testament I will make choice of that memorable event on which the salvation of believers in every age rests as its foundation, the death and sufferings of the Son of God. This the great adversary and all his

---

* The matter is fully stated and reasoned upon by the prophet Isaiah ch. x. from the 5th to the 19th verse.

John Witherspoon

agents and instruments prosecuted with unrelenting rage. When they had blackened him with slander, when they scourged him with shame, when they had condemned him in judgment, and nailed him to the cross, how could they help esteeming their victory complete? But oh the unsearchable wisdom of God! they were but perfecting the great design laid for the salvation of sinners. Our blessed Redeemer by his death finished his work, overcame principalities and powers, and made a shew of them openly, triumphing over them in his cross. With how much justice do the apostles and their company offer this doxology to God, "They lift up their voice with one accord, and said, Lord thou art God which hast made heaven and earth, and the sea, and all that in them is; Who by the mouth of thy servant David hast said, Why did the Heathen rage, and the people imagine vain things? The kings of the earth stood up, and the rulers were gathered together against the Lord, and against his Christ. For of a truth, against thy holy child Jesus, whom thou hast anointed, both Herod and Pontius Pilate, with the Gentiles, and the people of Israel were gathered together, for to do whatsoever thy hand and thy counsel determined before to be done." Acts iv. 24. 28.

In all after ages, in conformity to this, the deepest laid contrivances of the prince of darkness, have turned out to the confusion of their author; and I know not, but considering his malice and pride, this perpetual disappointment, and the superiority of divine wisdom, may be one great source of his suffering and torment. The cross hath still been the banner of truth, under which it hath been carried through the world. Persecution has been but as the furnace to the gold, to purge it of its dross, to manifest its purity, and increase its lustre. It was taken notice of very early, that the blood of the martyrs was the seed of christianity; the more abundantly it was shed, the more plentifully did the harvest grow.

So certain has this appeared, that the most violent infidels, both of early and later ages, have endeavored to account for it, and have observed that there is a spirit of obstinacy in man which inclines him to resist violence, and that severity doth but increase opposition, be the cause what it will. They suppose that persecution is equally proper to propagate truth and error. This though in part true, will by no means generally hold. Such an apprehension, however, gave occasion to a glorious triumph of divine providence of an opposite kind, which I must shortly relate to you. One of the

Roman emperors, Julian, surnamed the apostate, perceiving how impossible it was to suppress the gospel by violence, endeavored to extinguish it by neglect and scorn. He left the Christians unmolested for sometime, but gave all manner of encouragement to those of opposite principles, and particularly to the Jews, out of hatred to the Christians; and that he might bring public disgrace upon the Galileans, as he affected to stile them, he encouraged the Jews to rebuild the temple of Jerusalem, and visibly refute the prophecy of Christ, that it should lie under perpetual desolation. But this profane attempt was so signally frustrated, that it served, as much as any one circumstance, to spread the glory of our Redeemer, and establish the faith of his saints. It is affirmed by some ancient authors, particularly by Ammianus Marcellinus, a heathen historian, that fire came out of the earth and consumed the workmen when laying the foundation. But in whatever way it was prevented, it is beyond all controversy, from the concurring testimony of heathens and Christians, that little or no progress was ever made in it, and that in a short time, it was entirely defeated.

It is proper here to observe, that at the time of the reformation, when religion began to revive, nothing contributed more to facilitate its reception and increase its progress than the violence of its persecutors. Their cruelty and the patience of the sufferers, naturally disposed men to examine and weigh the cause to which they adhered with so much constancy and resolution. At the same also, when they were persecuted in one city, they fled to another, and carried the discoveries of popish fraud to every part of the world. It was by some of those who were persecuted in Germany, that the light of reformation was brought so early into Britain.

The power of divine providence appears with the most distinguished lustre, when small and inconsiderable circumstances, and sometimes, the weather and seasons, have defeated the most formidable armaments, and frustrated the best concerted expeditions. Near two hundred years ago, the monarchy of Spain was in the height of its power and glory, and determined to crush the interest of the reformation. They sent out a powerful armament against Britain, giving it ostentatiously, and in my opinion profanely, the name of the Invincible Armada. But it pleased God so entirely to discomfit it by tempests, that a small part of it returned home, though no British force had been opposed to it at all.

We have a remarkable instance of the influence of small circumstance in providence in the English history. The two most remarkable persons in the civil wars, had earnestly desired to withdraw themselves from the contentions of the times, Mr. Hampden and Oliver Cromwell. They had actually taken their passage in a ship for New England, when by an arbitrary order of council they were compelled to remain at home. The consequence of this was, that one of them was the soul of the republican opposition to monarchical usurpation during the civil wars, and the other in the course of that contest, was the great instrument in bringing the tyrant to the block.

The only other historical remark I am to make, is, that the violent persecution which many eminent Christians met with in England from their brethren, who called themselves Protestants, drove them in great numbers to a distant part of the world, where the light of the gospel and true religion were unknown. Some of the American settlements, particularly those in New-England, were chiefly made by them; and as they carried the knowledge of Christ to the dark places of the earth, so they continue themselves in as great a degree of purity, of faith, and strictness of practice, or rather a greater, than is to be found in any protestant church now in the world. Does not the wrath of man in this instance praise God? Was not the accuser of the brethren, who stirs up their enemies, thus taken in his own craftiness, and his kingdom shaken by the very means which he employed to establish it.*

II. Proceed now to the second general head, which was to apply the principles illustrated above to our present situation, by inferences of truth for your instruction and comfort, and by suitable exhortations to duty in this important crisis. And,

In the first place, I would take the opportunity on this occasion, and from this subject, to press every hearer to a sincere concern for his own soul's salvation. There are times when the mind may be expected to be more awake to divine truth, and the conscience more open to the arrows of conviction, than at others. A season of public judgment is of this kind, as appears from what has been already said. That curiosity and attention at least are raised in some degree, is plain from the unusual throng of this assembly. Can you have a clearer view of the sinfulness of your nature, than when the rod of the oppressor is lifted up, and when you see men putting on the habit of the warrior, and collecting on every hand the weapons of hostility and instruments of death? I do not blame your ardor in preparing for the resolute defence of your temporal rights. But consider I beseech

---

* Lest this should be thought a temporising compliment to the people of New England, who have been the first sufferers in the present contest, and have set so noble an example of invincible fortitude, in withstanding the violence of oppression, I think it proper to observe that the whole paragraph is copied from a sermon on Psal. lxxiv. 22. prepared and preached in Scotland, in the month of August, 1758.

you, the truly infinite importance of the salvation of your souls. Is it of much moment whether you and your children shall be rich or poor, at liberty or in bonds? Is it of much moment whether this beautiful country shall increase in fruitfulness from year to year, being cultivated by active industry, and possessed by independent freemen, or the scanty produce of the neglected fields shall be eaten up by hungry publicans, while the timid owner trembles at the tax gatherers approach? And is it of less moment my brethren, whether you shall be the heirs of glory or the heirs of hell? Is your state on earth for a few fleeting years of so much moment? And is it of less moment, what shall be your state through endless ages? Have you assembled together willingly to hear what shall be said on public affairs, and to join in imploring the blessing of God on the counsels and arms of the united colonies, and can you be unconcerned, what shall become of you for ever, when all the monuments of human greatness shall be laid in ashes, for "the earth *itself* and all the works that are therein shall be burnt up."

Wherefore my beloved hearers, as the ministry of reconciliation is committed to me, I beseech you in the most earnest manner, to attend to "the things that belong to your peace, before they are hid from your eyes." How soon and in what manner a seal shall be set upon the character and state of every person here present, it is impossible to know; for he who only can know does not think proper to reveal it. But you may rest assured that there is no time more suitable, and there is none so safe, as that which is present, since it is wholly uncertain whether any other shall be your's. Those who shall first fall in battle, have not many more warnings to receive. There are some few daring and hardened sinners who despise eternity itself, and set their Maker at defiance, but the far greater number by staving off their convictions to a more convenient season, have been taken unprepared, and thus eternally lost. I would therefore earnestly press the apostles exhortation; 2 Cor. vi. I, 2. "We then, as workers together with him, beseech you also, that ye receive not the grace of God in vain: For he saith, I have heard thee in a time accepted, and in the day of salvation have I succoured thee: Behold, now is the accepted time; behold, now is the day of salvation."

Suffer me to beseech you, or rather to give you warning, not to rest satisfied with a form of godliness, denying the power thereof. There can be no true religion, till there be a discovery of your lost state by nature and practice, and an unfeigned acceptance of Christ Jesus, as he is offered in the

John Witherspoon

gospel. Unhappy they who either despise his mercy, or are ashamed of his cross! Believe it, "there is no salvation in any other. There is no other name under heaven given amongst men by which we must be saved." Unless you are united to him by a lively faith, not the resentment of a haughty monarch, but the sword of divine justice hangs over you, and the fulness of divine vengeance shall speedily overtake you. I do not speak this only to the heaven daring profligate, or grovelling sensualist, but to every insensible secure sinner; to all those, however decent and orderly in their civil deportment, who live to themselves and have their part and portion in this life; in fine to all who are yet in a state of nature, for "except a man be born again, he cannot see the kingdom of God." The fear of man may make you hide your profanity: prudence and experience may make you abhor intemperance and riot; as you advance in life, one vice may supplant another and hold its place; but nothing less than the sovereign grace of God can produce a saving change of heart and temper, or fit you for his immediate presence.

2. From what has been said upon this subject, you may see what ground there is to give praise to God for his favors already bestowed on us, respecting the public cause. It would be a criminal inattention not to observe the singular interposition of Providence hitherto, in behalf of the American colonies. It is however impossible for me, in a single discourse, as well as improper at this time, to go through every step of our past transactions, I must therefore content myself with a few remarks. How many discoveries have been made of the designs of enemies in Britain and among ourselves, in a manner as unexpected to us as to them, and in such season as to prevent their effect? What surprising success has attended our encounters in almost every instance? Has not the boasted discipline of regular and veteran soldiers been turned into confusion and dismay, before the new and maiden courage of freeman, in defence of their property and right? In what great mercy has blood been spared on the side of this injured country? Some important victories in the south have been gained with so little loss, that enemies will probably think it has been dissembled; as many, even of ourselves thought, till time rendered it undeniable. But these were comparatively of small moment. The signal advantage we have gained by the evacuation of Boston, and the shameful flight of the army and navy of Britain, was brought about without the loss of a man. To all this we may add, that the counsels of our enemies have been visibly confounded, so that

I believe that I may say with truth, that there is hardly any step which they have taken, but it has operated strongly against themselves, and been more in our favor, than if they had followed a contrary course.

While we give praise to God the supreme disposer of all events, for his interposition in our behalf, let us guard against the dangerous error of trusting in, or boasting of an arm of flesh. I could earnestly wish, that while our arms are crowned with success, we might content ourselves with a modest ascription of it to the power of the Highest. It has given me great uneasiness to read some ostentatious, vaunting expressions in our news-papers, though happily I think, much restrained of late. Let us not return to them again. If I am not mistaken, not only the holy scriptures in general, and the truths of the glorious gospel in particular, but the whole course of providence, seem intended to abase the pride of man, and lay the vain-glorious in the dust. How many instances does history furnish us with, of those who after exulting over, and despising their enemies, were signally and shamefully defeated.* The truth is, I believe, the remark may be applied universally, and we may say, that through the whole frame of nature, and the whole system of human life, that which promises most, performs the least. The flowers of finest colour seldom have the sweetest fragrance. The trees of quickest groweth or fairest form, are seldom of the greatest value or duration. Deep waters move with least noise. Men who think most are seldom talkative. And I think it holds as much in war as in any thing, that every boaster is a coward.

Pardon me, my brethren, for insisting so much upon this, which may seem but an immaterial circumstance. It is in my opinion of very great moment. I look upon ostentation and confidence to be a sort of outrage upon Providence, and when it becomes general, and infuses itself into the spirit of a people, it is a forerunner of destruction. How does Goliath the champion armed in a most formidable manner, express his disdain of David the stripling with his sling and his stone, 1 Sam. xvii 42, 43, 44, 45. "And when the Philistine looked about and saw David, he disdained him: for he was but a youth, and ruddy, and of a fair countenance. And the Philistine said unto David, Am I a dog, that thou comest to me with staves? And the Philistine cursed David by his gods, and the Philistine said to David, come to me, and I will give thy flesh unto the fowls of the air, and to the beasts of the field." But how just and modest the reply? ["]Then said David to

---

*There is no story better known in British history, than that the officers of the French army the night preceding the battle of Agincourt, played at dice for English prisoners before they took them, and the next day were taken by them.

John Witherspoon

the Philistine, thou comest to me with a sword and with a spear, and with a shield, but I come unto thee in the name of the Lord of hosts, the God of the armies of Israel, whom thou hast defied." I was well pleased with a remark of this kind thirty years ago in a pamphlet,* in which it was observed, that there was great deal of profane ostentation in the names given to ship of war, as the Victory, the Valiant, the Thunderer, the Dreadnought, the Terrible, the Firebrand, the Furnace, the Lightning, the Infernal, and many more of the same kind. This the author considered as a symptom of the national character and manners very unfavorable, and not likely to obtain the blessing of the God of heaven.†

3. From what has been said you may learn what encouragement you have to put your trust in God, and hope for his assistance in the present important conflict. He is the Lord of hosts, great in might, and strong in battle. Whoever hath his countenance and approbation shall have the best at last. I do not mean to speak prophetically, but agreeably to the analogy of faith, and the principals of God's moral government. Some have observed that true religion, and in her train, dominion, riches, literature, and arts, have taken their course in a slow and gradual manner, from east to west, since the earth was settled after the flood, and from thence forebode the future glory of America. I leave this as a matter rather of conjecture than certainty, but observe, that if your cause is just, if your principles are pure, and if your conduct is prudent, you need not fear the multitude of opposing hosts.

If your cause is just – you may look with confidence to the Lord and intreat him to plead it as his own. You are all my witnesses, that this is the first time of my introducing any political subject into the pulpit. At this season however, it is not only lawful but necessary, and I willingly embrace the opportunity of declaring my opinion without any hesitation, that the cause in which America is now in arms, is the cause of justice, of liberty, and of human nature. So far as we have hitherto proceeded, I am satisfied that the confederacy of the colonies, has not been the effect of pride, resentment, or sedition, but of a deep and general conviction, that our civil

---

*Britain's Remembrancer.

†I am sensible that one or two of these were ships taken from the French, which brought their names with them. But the greatest number had their names imposed in England, and I cannot help observing, that the Victory, often celebrated as the finest ship ever built in Britain, was lost in the night without a storm, by some unknown accident, and about twelve hundred persons, many of them of the first families in the nation, were buried with it in the deep. I do not mean to infer any thing from this, but, that we ought to live under the practical persuasion of what no man will doctrinally deny, that there is no warring with the elements, or him who directs their force; that he is able to write disappointment on the wisest human schemes, and by the word of his power to frustrate the efforts of the greatest monarch upon earth.

and religious liberties, and consequently in a great measure the temporal and eternal happiness of us and our posterity, depended on the issue. The knowledge of God and his truths have from the beginning of the world been chiefly, if not entirely, confined to those parts of the earth where some degree of liberty and political justice were to be seen, and great were the difficulties with which they had to struggle from the imperfection of human society, and the unjust decisions of usurped authority. There is not a single instance in history in which civil liberty was lost, and religious liberty preserved entire. If therefore we yield up our temporal property, we at the same time deliver the conscience into bondage.

You shall not, my brethren, hear from me in the pulpit, what you have never heard from me in conversation, I mean railing at the king personally, or even his ministers and the parliament, and people of Britain, as so many barbarous savages. Many of their actions have probably been worse than their intentions. That they should desire unlimited dominion, if they can obtain or preserve it, is neither new nor wonderful. I do not refuse submission to their unjust claims, because they are corrupt or profligate, although probably many of them are so, but because they are men, and therefore liable to all the selfish bias inseparable from human nature. I call this claim unjust, of making laws to bind us in all cases whatsoever, because they are separated from us, independent of us, and have an interest in opposing us.

Would any man who could prevent it, give up his estate, person, and family, to the disposal of his neighbour, although he had liberty to chuse the wisest and the best master? Surely not.

This is the true and proper hinge of the controversy between Great-Britain and America. It is however to be added, that such is their distance from us, that a wise and prudent administration of our affairs is as impossible as the claim of authority is unjust. Such is and must be their ignorance of the state of things here, so much time must elapse before an error can be seen and remedied, and so much injustice and partiality must be expected from the arts and misrepresentation of interested persons, that for these colonies to depend wholly upon the legislature of Great-Britain, would be like many other oppressive connexions, injury to the master, and ruin to the slave.

The management of the war itself on their part, would furnish new proof of this, if any were needful. Is it not manifest with what absurdity and impropriety they have conducted their own designs? We had nothing so much to fear as dissension, and they have by wanton and unnecessary cruelty forced us into union. At the same time to let us see what we have to expect, and what would be the fatal consequence of unlimited submission, they have uniformly called those acts *Lenity*, which filled this whole continent with resentment and horror. The ineffable disdain expressed by our fellow subject, in saying, "That he would not hearken to America, till she was at his feet," has armed more men, and inspired more deadly rage, than could have been done by laying waste a whole province with fire and sword. Again we wanted not numbers, but time, and they sent over handful after handful till we were ready to oppose a multitude greater than they have to send. In fine, if there was one place stronger than the rest, and more able and willing to resist, there they made the attack, and left the others till they were duly informed, completely incensed, and fully furnished with every instrument of war.

I mention these things, my brethren, not only as grounds of confidence in God, who can easily overthrow the wisdom of the wise, but as decisive proofs of the impossibility of these great and growing states, being safe and happy when every part of their internal polity is dependant on Great Britain. If, on account of their distance, and ignorance of our situation, they could not conduct their own quarrel with propriety for one year, how can they give direction and vigor to every department of our civil constitutions from age to age? There are fixed bounds to every human thing. When branches of a tree grow very large and weighty, they fall off from the trunk. The sharpest sword will not pierce when it cannot reach. And there is a certain distance from the seat of government, where an attempt to rule will either produce tyranny and helpless subjection, or provoke resistance and effect a separation.

I have said, if your principles are pure – the meaning of this is, if your present opposition to the claims of the British ministry does not arise from a seditious and turbulent spirit, or a wanton contempt of legal authority; from a blind and factious attachment to particular persons or parties; or from a selfish rapacious disposition, and a desire to turn public confusion to private profit – but from a concern for the interest of your country, and the safety of yourselves and your posterity. On this subject I cannot help observing, that though it would be a miracle if there were not many selfish persons among us, and discoveries now and then made of mean and interested transactions, yet they have been comparatively inconsiderable both in number and effect. In general, there has been so great a degree of public spirit, that we have much more reason to be thankful for its vigor and prevalence, than to wonder at the few appearances of dishonesty or disaffection. It would be very uncandid to ascribe the universal ardor that has prevailed among all ranks of men, and the spirited exertions in the most distant colonies, to any thing else than public spirit. Nor was there ever perhaps in history so general a commotion from which religious differences have been so entirely excluded. Nothing of this kind has yet been heard, except of late in the absurd, but malicious and detestable attempts of our few remaining enemies to introduce them. At the same time I must also, for the honor of this country observe, that though government in the ancient forms has been so long unhinged, and in some colonies not sufficient care taken to substitute another in its place; yet has there been, by common consent, a much greater degree of order and public peace, than men of reflection and experience foretold or expected. From all these circumstances I conclude favorably of the principles of the friends of liberty, and do earnestly exhort you to adopt and act upon those which have been described, and resist the influence of every other.

Once more, if to the justice of your cause, and the purity of your principles, you add prudence in your conduct, there will be the greatest reason to hope, by the blessing of God, for prosperity and success. By prudence in conducting this important struggle, I have chiefly in view union, firmness, and patience. Every body must perceive the absolute necessity of union. It is indeed in every body's mouth, and therefore instead of attempting to convince you of its importance, I will only caution you against the usual causes of division. If persons of every rank, instead of implicitly complying with the orders of those whom they themselves have chosen to direct, will needs judge every measure over again, when it comes to be put in execution; if different classes of men intermix their little private views, or clashing interest with public affairs, and marshal into parties, the merchant against the landholder, and the landholder against the merchant; if local provincial pride and jealousy arise, and you allow yourselves to speak with contempt of the courage, character, manners, or even language of particular places, you are doing a greater injury to the common cause, than you are aware of. If such practices are admitted among us, I shall look upon it as one of the most dangerous symptoms, and if they become general, a

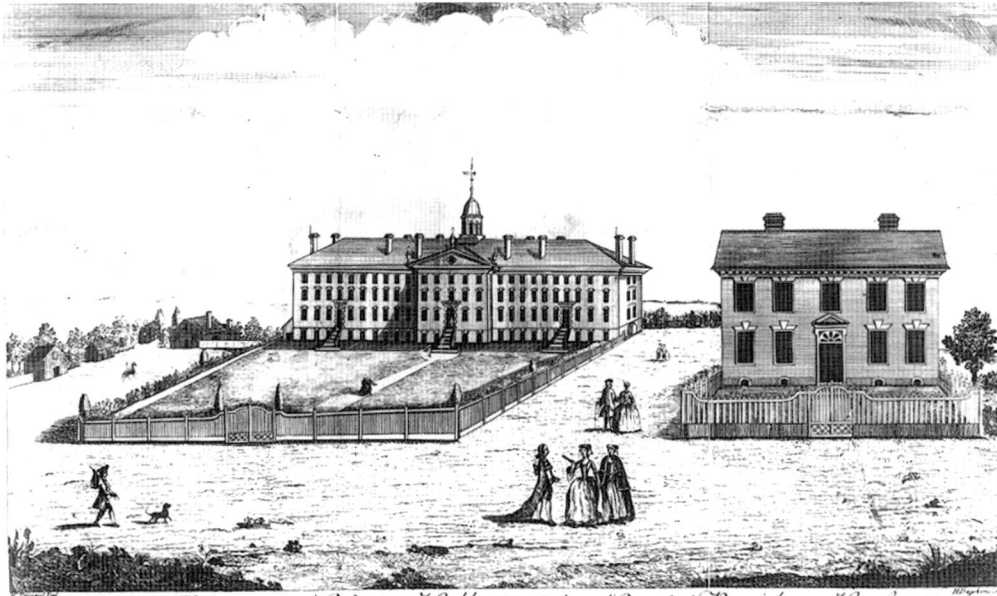

. A North-West Prospect of Nassau-Hall, with a Front View of the Presidents House, in New Jersey

Nassau Hall was the location for one of Witherspoon's best-remembered sermons, titled "The Dominion of Providence Over the Passions of Men," in which he clearly articulated his pro-independence stance. To the right of the Hall is the McLean House, Witherspoon's campus residence.

presage of approaching ruin.

By firmness and patience, I mean a resolute adherence to your duty, and laying your account with many difficulties, as well as occasional disappointments. In a former part of this discourse, I have cautioned you against ostentation and vain glory. Be pleased farther to observe that extremes often beget one another, the same persons who exult extravagantly on success, are generally most liable to despondent timidity on every little inconsiderable defeat. Men of this character are the bane and corruption of every society or party to which they belong, but they are especially the ruin of an army, if suffered to continue in it. Remember the vicissitude of human things, and the usual course of providence. How often has a just cause been reduced to the lowest ebb, and yet when firmly adhered to, has become finally triumphant. I speak this now while the affairs of the colonies are in so prosperous a state, lest this prosperity itself should render you less able to bear unexpected misfortunes – the sum of the whole is, that the blessing of God is only to be looked for by those who are not wanting in the discharge of their own duty. I would neither have you to trust in an arm of flesh, nor sit with folded hands and expect that miracles should be wrought in your defence – this is a sin which is in scripture stiled tempting God. In opposition to it, I would exhort you as Joab did the host of Israel, who, though he does not appear to have had a spotless character throughout, certainly in this instance spoke like a prudent general and a pious man. 2 Sam. x. 12. "Be of good courage, and let us behave ourselves valiantly for our people and for the cities of our God, and let the Lord do that which is good in his sight."

I shall now conclude this discourse by some exhortations to duty, founded upon the truths which have been illustrated above, and suited to the interesting state of this country at the present time; and,

I. Suffer me to recommend to you an attention to the public interest of religion, or in other words, zeal for the glory of God and the good of others. I have already endeavored to exhort sinners to repentance; what I have here in view is to point out to you the concern which every good man ought to take in the national character and manners, and the means which he ought to use for promoting public virtue, and bearing down impiety and vice. This is a matter of the utmost moment, and which ought to be well understood, both in its nature and principles. Nothing is more certain than that a general profligacy and corruption of manners make a people ripe for destruction. A good form of government may hold the rotten materials together for some time; but beyond certain pitch, even the best constitution will be ineffectual and slavery must ensue. On the other hand, when the manners of a nation are pure, when true religion and internal principles maintain their vigor, the attempts of the most powerful enemies to oppress them are commonly baffled and disappointed. This will be found equally certain, whether we consider the great principles of God's moral government, or the operation and influence of natural causes.

What follows from this? That he is the best friend to American liberty, who is most sincere and active in promoting true and undefiled religion, and who sets himself with the greatest firmness to bear down profanity and immorality of every kind. Whoever is an avowed enemy to God, I scruple not to call him an enemy to his country. Do not suppose, my brethren, that I mean to recommend a furious and angry zeal for the circumstantials of religion; or the contentions of one sect with another about their peculiar distinctions. I do not wish you to oppose any body's religion, but every body's wickedness. Perhaps there are few surer marks of the reality of religion, than when a man feels himself more joined in spirit to a true holy person of a different denomination, than to an irregular liver of his own. It is therefore your duty in this important and critical season to exert yourselves, every one in his proper sphere, to stem the tide of prevailing vice, to promote the knowledge of God, the reverence of his name and worship, and obedience to his laws.

Perhaps you will ask, what it is that you are called to do for this purpose farther than your own personal duty? I answer this itself when taken in its proper extent is not a little. The nature and obligation of visible religion is, I am afraid, little understood and less attended to.

Many from a real or pretended fear of the imputation of hypocrisy, banish from their conversation and carriage every appearance of respect and submission to the living God. What a weakness and meanness of spirit does it discover, for a man to be ashamed in the presence of his fellow sinners, to profess that reverence to almighty God which he inwardly feels: The truth is, he makes himself truly liable to the accusation which he means to avoid. It is as genuine and perhaps a more culpable hypocrisy to appear to have less religion than you really have, than to appear to have more. This false shame is a more extensive evil than is commonly apprehended. We contribute constantly, though insensibly, to form each others character and manners; and therefore, the usefulness of a strictly holy and conscientious deportment is not confined to the possessor, but spreads its happy influence to all that are within its reach. I need scarcely add, that in proportion as men are distinguished by understanding, literature, age, rank, office, wealth, or any other circumstance, their example will be useful on the one hand, or pernicious the other.

But I cannot content myself with barely recommending a silent example. There is a dignity in virtue which is entitled to authority, and ought to claim it. In many cases it is the duty of a good man, by open reproof and opposition, to wage war with profaneness. There is a scripture precept delivered in very singular terms, to which I beg your attention; "Thou shalt not hate thy brother in thy heart, but shalt in any wise rebuke him, and not suffer sin upon him." How prone are many to represent reproof as flowing from ill nature and surliness of temper? The Spirit of God, on the contrary, considers it as the effect of inward hatred, or want of genuine love, to forbear reproof, when it is necessary or may be useful. I am sensible there may in some cases be a restraint from prudence, agreeably to that caution of our Saviour, "Cast not your pearls before swine, lest they trample them under their feet and turn again and rent you." Of this every man must judge as well as he can for himself; but certainly, either by open reproof, or expressive silence, or speedy departure from such society, we ought to guard against being partakers of other men's sins.

To this let me add, that if all men are bound in some degree, certain classes of men are under peculiar obligations, to the discharge of this duty. Magistrates, ministers, parents, heads of families, and those whom age has rendered venerable, are called to use their authority and influence for the glory of God and the good of others. Bad men themselves discover an inward conviction of this, for they are often liberal in their reproaches of persons of grave characters or religious profession, if they bear with patience the profanity of others. Instead of enlarging on the duty of men in authority in general, I must particularly recommend this matter to those who have the command of soldiers inlisted for the defence of their country. This cause is sacred, and the champions for it ought to be holy. Nothing is more grieving to the heart of a good man, than to hear from those who are going to the field, the horrid sound of cursing and blasphemy; it cools the ardor of his prayers, as well as abates his confidence and hope in God. Many more circumstances affect me in such a case, than I can enlarge upon, or indeed easily enumerate at present; the glory of God, the interest of the deluded sinner, going like a devoted victim, and imprecating vengeance on his own head, as well as the cause itself committed to his care. We have sometimes taken the liberty to forebode the downfall of the British empire, from the corruption and degeneracy of the people. Unhappily the British soldiers have been distinguished among all the nations in Europe, for the most shocking profanity. Shall we then pretend to emulate them in this internal distinction, or rob them of the horrid privilege? God forbid. Let the officers of the army in every degree remember, that as military subjection, while it lasts, is the most complete of any, it is in their power greatly to restrain, if not to wholly to banish, this flagrant enormity.

2. I exhort all who are not called to go into the field, to apply themselves with the utmost diligence to works of industry. It is in your power by this mean not only to supply the necessities, but to add to the strength of your country. Habits of industry prevailing in society, not only increase its wealth, as their immediate effect, but they prevent the introduction of

many vices, and are intimately connected with sobriety and good morals. Idleness is the mother or nurse of almost every vice; and want, which is its inseparable companion, urges men on to the most abandoned and destructive courses. Industry, therefore is a moral duty of the greatest moment, absolutely necessary to national prosperity, and the sure way of obtaining the blessing of God. I would also observe, that in this, as in every other part of God's government, obedience to his will is as much a natural mean, as a meritorious cause, of the advantage we wish to reap from it. Industry brings up a firm and hardy race. He who is inured to the labor of the field, is prepared for the fatigues of a campaign. The active farmer who rises with the dawn and follows his team or plow, must in the end be an overmatch for those effeminate and delicate soldiers, who nursed in the lap of self-indulgence, and whose greatest exertion is in the important preparation for, and tedious attendance on, a masquerade, or midnight ball.

3. In the last place, suffer me to recommend to you frugality in your families, and every other article of expence. This the state of things among us renders absolutely necessary, and it stands in the most immediate connexion both with virtuous industry, and active public spirit. Temperance in meals, moderation and decency in dress, furniture and equipage, have, I think, generally been characteristics of a distinguished patriot. And when the same spirit pervades a people in general, they are fit for every duty, and able to encounter the most formidable enemy. The general subject of the preceding discourse has been the wrath of man praising God. If the unjust oppression of your enemies, which withholds from you many of the usual articles of luxury and magnificence, shall contribute to make you clothe yourselves and your children with the works of your own hands, and cover your tables with the salutary productions of your own soil, it will be a new illustration of the same truth, and a real happiness to yourselves and your country.

I could wish to have every good thing done from the purest principles and the noblest views. Consider, therefore, that the Christian character, particularly the self-denial of the gospel, should extend to your whole deportment. In the early times of Christianity, when adult converts were admitted to baptism they were asked among other questions, Do you renounce the world, its shews, its pomp, and its vanities? I do. The form of this is still preserved in the administration of baptism, where we renounce the devil, the world, and the flesh. This certainly implies not only abstaining from acts of gross intemperance and excess, but a humility of carriage, a restraint and moderation in all your desires. The same thing, as it is suitable to your Christian profession, is also necessary to make you truly independent in yourselves, and to feed the source of liberality and charity to others, or to the public. The riotous and wasteful liver, whose craving appetites make him constantly needy, is and must be subject to many masters, according to the sayings of Solomon, "The borrower is servant to the lender." But the frugal and moderate person, who guides his affairs with discretion, is able to assist in public counsels by a free and unbiased judgement, to supply the wants of his poor brethren, and sometimes, by his estate and substance to give important aid to a sinking country.

Upon the whole, I beseech you to make a wise improvement of the present threatening aspect of public affairs, and to remember that your duty to God, to your country, to your families, and to yourselves, is the same. True religion is nothing else but an inward temper and outward conduct suited to your state and circumstances in providence at any time. And as peace with God and conformity to him, adds to the sweetness of created comforts while we possess them, so in times of difficulty and trial, it is in the man of piety and inward principle, that we may expect to find the uncorrupted patriot, the useful citizen, and the invincible soldier. God grant that in America true religion and civil liberty may be inseparable, and that the unjust attempts to destroy the one, may in the issue tend to the support and establishment of both.

Witherspoon's admonishment in one of his most well-known sermons:"Upon the whole, I beseech you to make a wise improvement of the present threatening aspect of public affairs, and to remember that your duty to God, to your country, to your families, and to yourselves, is the same."

University Archives. Department of Rare Books and Special Collections. Princeton University Library.

In CONGRESS.

DECEMBER 11, 1776.

WHEREAS, the juſt War into which the United States of America have been forced by Great-Britain, is likely to be ſtill continued by the ſame Violence and Injuſtice which have hitherto animated the Enemies of American Freedom : And, whereas it becomes all public Bodies, as well as private Perſons, to reverence the Providence of God, and look up to him as the ſupreme Diſpoſer of all Events, and the Arbiter of the Fate of Nations : Therefore the CONGRESS hereby RESOLVE,

That it be recommended to all the States, as ſoon as Poſſible to appoint a Day of ſolemn Faſting and Humiliation, to implore of Almighty GOD the Forgiveneſs of the many Sins prevailing among all Ranks, and to beg the Countenance and Aſſiſtance of his Providence in the Proſecution of this juſt and neceſſary War. The *Congreſs* do alſo in the moſt earneſt manner recommend to all the Members of the *United States*, and particularly to the Officers civil and military under them, the Exerciſe of Repentance and Reformation ; and further, do require of the ſaid Officers of the military Department, the ſtrict Obſervation of the Articles of War in general, and particularly that of ſaid articles which forbids profane Swearing, and all other Immoralities ; of which all ſuch Officers are deſired to take Notice. It is left to each State to iſſue Proclamations fixing the Day that appear moſt proper for their ſeveral Bounds.

Extract from the Minutes,

CHARLES THOMPSON, Secretary.

Hartford : Re-Printed by EBEN. WATSON.

During the early and uncertain days of the newly formed republic, it was not uncommon for the Continental Congress to issue public proclamations acknowledging and requesting divine intervention. Witherspoon penned this proclamation recommending that every citizen fast and request God's mercy and assistance in the war.

APPENDIX B

FAST DAY PROCLAMATION OF THE CONTINENTAL CONGRESS DECEMBER 11, 1776[81]

Whereas, the war in which the United States are engaged with Great Britain, has not only been prolonged, but is likely to be carried to the greatest extremity; and whereas, it becomes all public bodies, as well as private persons, to reverence the Providence of God, and look up to him as the supreme disposer of all events, and the arbiter of the fate of nations; therefore,

Resolved, That it be recommended to all the United States, as soon as possible, to appoint a day of solemn fasting and humiliation; to implore of Almighty God the forgiveness of the many sins prevailing among all ranks, and to beg the countenance as assistance of his Providence in the prosecution of the present just and necessary war.

The Congress do also, in the most earnest manner, recommend to all the members of the United States, and particularly the officers civil and military under them, the exercise of repentance and reformation; and further, require of them the strict observation of the articles of war, and particularly, that part of the said articles, which forbids profane swearing, and all immorality, of which all such officers are desired to take notice.

It is left to each State to issue out proclamations fixing the days that appear most proper within their several bounds.

---

[81] *The Journals of the Continental Congress*, 1774-1789, Worthington C. Ford, Gaillard Hunt, *et al.*, eds. (Washington, D.C.: Government Printing Office, 1904-37), Vol. 6, p. 1022.

Witherspoon's early draft of his congressional Thanksgiving Day Proclamation of October 26, 1781.

APPENDIX C

"THANKSGIVING DAY PROCLAMATION" OF THE CONFEDERATION CONGRESS OCTOBER 26, 1781[82]

Whereas, it hath pleased Almighty God, the father of all mercies, remarkably to assist and support the United States of America in their important struggle for liberty, against the long continued efforts of a powerful nation: it is the duty of all ranks to observe and thankfully acknowledge the interpositions of his Providence in their behalf. Through the whole of the contest, from its first rise to this time, the influence of Divine Providence may be clearly perceived in many signal instances, of which we mention but a few.

In revealing the councils of our enemies, when the discoveries were seasonable and important, and the means seemingly inadequate or fortuitous; in preserving and even improving the union of the several States, on the breach of which our enemies placed their greatest dependence; in increasing the number and adding to the zeal and attachment of the friends of Liberty; in granting remarkable deliverances, and blessing us with the most signal success, when affairs seemed to have the most discouraging appearance; in raising up for us a powerful and generous ally, in one of the first of the European powers; in confounding the councils of our enemies, and suffering them to pursue such measures as have most directly contributed to frustrate their own desires and expectations; above all, in making their extreme cruelty to the inhabitants of these States, when in their power, and their savage devastation of property, the very means of cementing our

---

[82] *Ibid.*, Vol. 21, pp. 1074-1076.

union, and adding vigor to every effort in opposition to them.

And as we cannot help leading the good people of these States to a retrospect on the events which have taken place since the beginning of the war, so we recommend in a particular manner to their observation, the goodness of God in the year now drawing to a conclusion; in which the Confederation of the United States has been completed; in which there have been so many instances of prowess and success in our armies; particularly in the Southern States, where, notwithstanding the difficulties with which they had to struggle, they have recovered the whole country which the enemy had overrun, leaving them only a post or two on or near the sea; in which we have been so powerfully and effectually assisted by our allies; in which in all the conjunct operations the most perfect harmony has subsisted in the allied army; in which there has been so plentiful a harvest, and so great abundance of the fruits of the earth of every kind, as not only enables us easily to supply the wants of the army, but gives comfort and happiness to the whole people; and in which, after the success of our allies by sea, a General of the first Rank, with his whole army, has been captured by the allied forces under the direction of our Commander in Chief.

It is therefore recommended to the several states to set apart the thirteenth day of December next, to be religiously observed as a Day of Thanksgiving and Prayer; that all the people may assemble on that day, with grateful hearts, to celebrate the praise of our gracious Benefactor; to confess our manifold sins; to offer up our most fervent supplications to the God of all grace, that it may please Him to pardon our offences, and incline our hearts for the future to keep all his laws; to comfort and relieve all our brethren who are in distress or captivity; to prosper all husbandmen, and give success to all engaged in lawful commerce; to impart wisdom and integrity to our counsellors, judgment and fortitude to our officers and soldiers; to protect and prosper our illustrious ally, and favor our united exertions for the speedy establishment of a safe, honorable and lasting peace; and bless all seminaries of learning; and cause the knowledge of God to cover the earth, as the water covers the seas.

John Witherspoon

An early version of another congressional Thanksgiving Day Proclamation, penned by Witherspoon in October 1782.

APPENDIX D

"THANKSGIVING DAY PROCLAMATION" OF THE CONFEDERATION CONGRESS OCTOBER 11, 1782[83]

It being the indispensable duty of all nations, not only to offer up their supplications to Almighty God, the giver of all good, for his gracious assistance in a time of distress, but also in a solemn and public manner to give him praise for his goodness in general, and especially for great and signal interpositions of his Providence in their behalf; therefore the United States in Congress assembled, taking into their consideration the many instances of divine goodness to these States, in the course of the important conflict in which they have been so long engaged; the present happy and promising state of public affairs; and the events of the war in the course of the year now drawing to a close, particularly the harmony of the public councils, which is so necessary to the success of the public cause; the perfect union and good understanding which has hitherto subsisted between them and their allies, notwithstanding the artful and unwearied attempts of the common enemy to divide them; the success of the armies of the United States and those of their allies, and the acknowledgment of their independence by another European power, whose friendship and commerce must be of great and lasting advantage to these States; do hereby recommend it to the inhabitants of these States in general, to observe, and request the several States to interpose their authority in appointing and commanding the observation of Thursday, the twenty-eighth day of November next, as a day of solemn thanksgiving to God for all his mercies; and they do further recommend to all ranks and testify their gratitude of God for his goodness, by a cheerful obedience to his laws, and by protecting, each in his station, and by his influence, the practice of true and undefiled religion, which is the great foundation of public prosperity and national happiness.

---

[83] *Ibid.*, Vol. 23, p. 647.

APPENDIX E
RECOMMENDED READING FOR FURTHER STUDY

Collins, Varnum Lansing. *President Witherspoon*. 2 vols. New York: Arno Press, 1969. Originally published by Princeton University Press in 1925, this work is the most scholarly and comprehensive biography available on Witherspoon.

Elazar, Daniel J. *Covenant & Constitutionalism: The Great Frontier and the Matrix of Federal Democracy*. New Brunswick, N.J.: Transaction Publishers, 1998. Written by a Jewish scholar at the Center of the Study of Federalism at Temple University, this work explores the biblical motif of covenant in the founding of the American republic. For those interested in exploring the Judeo-Christian religious roots of American political ideas, this work will prove helpful.

Noll, Mark A. *Princeton and the Republic, 1768-1822: The Search for a Christian Enlightenment in the Era of Samuel Stanhope Smith*. Princeton, N.J.: Princeton University Press, 1989. Noll offers a scholarly account of Princeton University's contribution to American political order as a hotbed of evangelical Calvinism and republicanism. The author critically explores the presidencies of Witherpoon, Samuel Stanhope Smith and Ashbel Green.

Olasky, Marvin. *Fighting For Liberty and Virtue: Political and Cultural Wars in Eighteenth-Century America*. Wheaton, Ill.: Crossway Books, 1995. This book is an insightful account of the religious, moral, cultural and political issues surrounding the events of the American Revolution.

Sandoz, Ellis. *A Government of Laws: Political Theory, Religion, and the American Founding*. Baton Rouge, La.: Louisiana State University Press, 1990. Sandoz provides a trenchant analysis of the religious and philosophical foundations of the American order. Witherspoon receives substantial scholarly attention in this work.